punctured preconceptions

what
north american
christians
think about
the church

Douglas W. Johnson
George W. Cornell

friendship press • new york
for
Section on Stewardship and Benevolence
National Council of the Churches of Christ in the U.S.A.

LIBRARY OF CHRISTIAN STEWARDSHIP

Handbook of Stewardship Procedures
 T. K. Thompson

Stewardship in Mission
 Winburn T. Thomas

The Christian Meaning of Money
 Otto A. Piper

Stewardship Illustrations
 T. K. Thompson

Why People Give
 Martin E. Carlson

Punctured Preconceptions
 Douglas W. Johnson and
 George W. Cornell

Copyright 1972 National Council of Churches
 Section on Stewardship and Benevolence

Library of Congress Cataloging in Publication Data
Johnson, Douglas W   1934-
 Punctured preconceptions.
 (Library of Christian stewardship)
 1. Church—Public opinion. 2. Public opinion—North
America. I. Cornell, George W., joint author. II. National Council of the Churches of Christ in the United
States of America. Section on Stewardship and Benevolence. III. Title.
BV600.2.J57   301.15'43'26097   72-6430
ISBN 0-377-32011-X

contents

FOR BOOK BORROWERS

FOR HIM that stealeth or borroweth and returneth not, this book from its owner, let it change into a serpent in his hand and rend him. Let him be struck with palsy and all his members be blasted. Let him languish in pain crying aloud for mercy, and let there be no surcease to his agony till he sink into dissolution. Let book-worms gnaw his entrails in token of the Worm that dieth not, and when at last he goeth to his final punishment, let the flames of Hell consume him for ever. ---

From the Monastery of San Pedro, Barcelona.

DENNIS G. FOTINOS

introduction

They carry fire on both shoulders, is a descriptive statement of church leaders who teach that the engines of the faith run on the resources shared by church members.

Called by God, through their denominations, stewardship leaders are responsible for resourcing the Church. Assigned the task of interpreting the most revolutionary of the churches' programs they do so with skill and dispatch and carry it to the most remote outpost. Called upon to raise money for salaries and floor wax, they engage with equal zeal and commitment. These dedicated leaders agreed that to continue their work, related to these exotic and mundane functions of the faith, without facts was increasing folly.

To know who the troops are, what they believe, their attitudes, how they are motivated, areas where they need help, how they feel about themselves and the church and the response they made was the course set by the North American Interchurch Study. *Punctured Preconceptions* is the report of this study to the church populace.

Wanting to feel the pulse of the church with their own hands, 150 national, regional and local stewardship workers ranged the U.S. and Canada.

Armed with 23 pages of questions they climbed the stairs of walk-up flats in the inner city and the dry creek beds of the Appalachian Mountains. They experienced the salty air of the

Maritimes and the arid air of Calgary. Feel the pulse they did! Three thousand four hundred and fifty of them, members all, from the periphery of local church life to the inner core.

Selected at random, interviewed at home, at work and over a cup of coffee at the local watering trough, they talked! This report is indicative of where the church is, what it believes, how it feels and what it hopes for the future. Those responsible for this in-depth study intend to use these indicators as directives for program development. The lode of information, still waiting to be mined from the computer, will continue to assist the leadership of the church to be more responsive to the reality of what the action is and where it is taking place.

Brought together through the Stewardship office of the National Council of the Churches of Christ in the U.S.A., 15 denominations provided human and financial resources for the study. These denominations are: The American Baptist Convention, The American Lutheran Church, Christian Church (Disciples of Christ), Church of God (Anderson, Indiana), Church of the Brethren, Cumberland Presbyterian Church, Lutheran Church in America, Lutheran Church—Missouri Synod, Mennonite Church, Reformed Church in America, Seventh-day Adventist Church, United Church of Canada, United Church of Christ, United Methodist Church, and the United Presbyterian Church in the U.S.A.

Some denominations elected to provide only money. These denominations are: The Anglican Church in Canada, The Churches of God in North America, Friends United Meeting, The Episcopal Church, General Conference Mennonite Church, Reorganized Church of Jesus Christ of Latter Day Saints, Moravian Church in America and The Presbyterian Church in Canada.

5

A core of stewardship executives and researchers gave credence to the study and deserve special mention. They are: James Baar, Earl Brewer, Gordon Danielson, Donald Goodger, Robert Hull, Lorenz Grumm, John Van Iderstine, David Lawson, James Lollis, Clifford Lott, Sheldon Mackey, A. C. McKee, Paul Picard, Kenneth Priebe, Ralph Rott, Orval Schmidt, Donald Stern, David Stone, Alan Waltz and Marvin Wilbur.

Staff, who gave second mile service and warrant special note are: Stanley Haidl, Bertie Meeker and Emma Saxlehner.

The interviewers, too numerous to mention by name, deserve a salute. To local pastors and church members, without whom the study could not have been made, deep felt gratitude is expressed.

To you, the reader, mover and shaker in the faith, we commend this report, to the end that it will give you new hope and deepen your commitment to the church and its work.

Nordan C. Murphy
Director for Stewardship in
the National Council of Churches
Project Administrator, Co-Director
and Editor

1.

spiking

some assumptions

An observer notices a stand of cottonwood trees along the edge of a wood and assumes they characterize the forest. His report gets around and soon most everyone considers the forest made up of cottonwood trees. It may be so or it may not. Whatever the case, this is how uncertainties become clothed with assumptions. It's a common, everyday device—useful, even necessary. It offers some basis for evaluation in the midst of constant unknowns. In order to function at all, says philosopher André Maurois, "we assume we understand things we do not actually understand."

Every society is loaded with assumptions born of plausibilities and piecemeal bits of evidence that have been extended by inference and repetition into broadly accepted generalizations. Sometimes they may be right, but as the record shows, they also can be monumentally wrong. It is when facts that plainly contradict the assumption are brought out that the whole collectively built-up frame of viewpoint comes tumbling down. The change may take place slowly or quickly, but when fallacy is shown up to be what it is, its grip is gone, its spell broken.

This has happened repeatedly in history. It also has happened in religious life. Findings brought out in this study suggest that in the case of many commonly held notions about the church and its people, the same sort of major reorientation needs to happen again. Those cottonwood trees have been camouflaging the church landscape.

The story of overturned ideas, reversed judgments and shattered illusions is an old one in human annals, and it goes on increasingly as methods of testing are refined and communications quicken and expand. Only in modern times has civilization begun to reshape its assumptions and laws about race, about the unrestrained drive to exploit nature, about colonialism, about rights of women. In rapid order, we have had to abandon previous assumptions that "ether" fills space, that cigarettes are harmless, that women must bear children in pain, that all motivations are conscious, that a Roman Catholic can't win the U. S. presidency. Contrary to past assumptions, we've had to recognize that light rays are not just waves but also something else, that energy and matter actually are of the same essence, that electronic pictures invisibly swarm the atmosphere, that time is not absolute, that interplanetary rockets are not just Buck Rogers fantasies. We've even had to shift the borderline of death from heartbeat to brainwaves.

As further realities come into focus, the once established assumptions go by the board, and views readjust to take the new factors into account. These reassessments have taken place in every field of knowledge, in organizations, nations, cultures. Each moves by a sequence of probabilities, further perceptions, corrections and new approaches. Religion is a running chronicle of such realignments and reappraisals —its early "illegal" phase, the church-state alliances, the monastic period, the Protestant Reformation, the modern ecumenical movement, Roman Catholicism's Second Vatican Council of

1962-65, which transformed its entire view and relationship to other churches.

Always there are those who resist the newly obvious situations, holding back, clinging to the old patterns, the past presumptions and fixed ideas, long after they have been outdated and left behind by new understandings and newly manifest conditions. Even after Neil Armstrong landed on the moon and sent back televised pictures of our terrestrial globe, Britain's Flat Earth Society continued to stick staunchly to its horizontal view of the world. It does look that way.

So it often has been with the church, sometimes mistakenly, sometimes for good reasons. As the custodian and disseminator of permanent values and principles, the church cannot live up to its job if it easily wavers and veers with each passing wind of ideological fashion. However, aside from its essential convictions, the church also is an organization, a functioning structure of congregations, agencies, administrators, methods, budgets and policies, designed to carry out its basic purposes and developed on the basis of inherited systems and generally assumed conditions, preferences and concerns of its people.

It is here on this operational level of sensing the intent, will and mood within its own constituency that the church, its leadership and its members, in many cases, have miscalculated the situation among themselves. According to information amassed in this study, considered the widest and most broadly probing ever made among North American Christians, their feelings and outlooks on many sensitive matters are far different from what generally has been supposed.

In short, the church, in its self-understanding, has misinterpreted the signs, drawn ill-founded implications about its own internal attitudes and urgencies. The discernible features of its real

9

character are there, stirring among its people and pastors, but these symptoms previously had not been sought out, compiled and analyzed to make them clear. The pulsebeat of the church-at-large had not been accurately gauged. Its wider voice had gone mostly unheard.

It was to catch the accents in that voice, to search out its prevailing tone, to unleash it and give it range, that this study was undertaken. Systematic depth interviews on current key problems, centered on the present degree of support for the church and the reasons for or against it, were conducted with 3,450 church members and pastors in a broad cross-section of denominations across the United States and Canada. The sampling, distributed geographically and by other categories based on information from the Bureau of the Census to make it representative of the entire population, was more than twice as large as that used in a Gallup poll. But it wasn't just a poll, but rather penetrating sessions of inquiry, sometimes lasting for two hours or more per person, and the filling out of 23 pages of answers. Twenty-three denominations provided funds and the 150 staff members who did the interviewing from coast to coast and from Saskatoon to Mobile.

Through this two-year, transcontinental colloquy, through this vast outpouring of personal sentiments and reactions from poor homes and rich, from backwoods cabins and metropolitan penthouses, from the young and old, from dubious backbench sitters and busy pillars of the congregations, from the bitter and the satisfied, each person telling it as he or she saw it. Thus the real church, from its heartland, had its say.

"I had a lot to get off my chest," one Pennsylvania farmer observed. "This is the first time the church has ever listened to me."

But if some were surprised at being heard, the picture that emerged of the church contained even more surprises. It just didn't fit the usual preconceptions. Somehow, the straight of the message hadn't been getting through. The word, the meanings, back and forth, among persons, pastors and denominations, apparently had often become crossed up, garbled and misconstrued. They seemed out of proportion, overdrawn, and in some cases, as measured by the findings, downright erroneous.

So extensively have they been held forth and echoed up and down the line in divergent forms and from various perspectives that most echelons in the church, including the people, have tended to consider them true, even though predominantly disavowing them. Ordinarily their breeding ground seems to have been the extent to which persons either were removed from a particular activity or closely associated with it. Somehow, out of that contrasting distance and proximity, with frequent broken circuits and static in between, the one-sided understandings have arisen, circulated and gradually attained currency. Often they contain half truths, fragments of it, yet only marginally, out of balance with the whole.

As a result, there have been misimpressions of the denominations, of the congregations, of the clergy, about attitudes in each, and even about the exposition of faith. These assumptions considerably influence the church in channeling its energies, its responses to the people and its general performance. Just as misreckonings can hamper its work and bend it off course, so may righting those reckonings help it chart its proper way and deal more ably with the realities. In that interest, this study was carried out.

The outcome means confronting the unexpected. Many of the modern clichés about North American church life just don't stand up.

To state briefly a few of the punctured balloons, the bulk of Christians on this continent want their denominations to speak out on social issues and to support minority groups. Contrary to the preconceptions, the hazards of grappling with social problems are more feared by the clergy than lay people, even though a somewhat larger proportion of clergy favor such activity despite their trepidations. Their anxieties turn out to be based partly on imagination.

It is generally supposed that an "uninformed" laity is much more likely than "informed" clergy to withhold funds from the church when they don't like its stand on some controversial issue, but this also is false. Only a tiny fraction of either clergy or laity have done it, and most of them disapprove of it. Official nervousness about their doing so and presumptions that they commonly use that tactic are largely illusory. However, church people do want a greater voice in how the church applies its funds.

The clergy also miscalculates the causes of people losing interest in the church, assuming it happens simply because the church has declined in importance for them. The laity strongly disagrees, saying the defections stem from their need, in the limited time they have, for more compelling, personally fulfilling fare. They don't want the church to function as a "social club," contrary to routine misconjectures that they do. They value the local church chiefly as a medium of evangelism, teaching, worship and service, and assert the importance to it of the denomination. However, they're more supportive of inter-denominational cooperation than the clergy, who are almost twice as likely to oppose ecumenical activity as lay people.

Also contradicting a virtual axiom of modern churchmanship that classic doctrines of Christianity need to be reinterpreted in contemporary terms, American Protestants today overwhelmingly affirm the traditional concepts of faith and insist that these be preached and taught, along with a vigorous effort to persuade others of Christ's saving truth. They're ready for struggle in the world, but they want the religious underpinnings for it, and they find that support in the Gospel, undiminished, undiluted and straight.

ASSUMPTIONS ABOUT THE DENOMINATION

One of the key themes of American folklore is the primacy of the locality, of the particular town and of the excelling virtues of the neighborhood and region. It has been asserted regularly in political slogans, "home rule," "state's rights," "federal encroachments," always in opposition to the ogre of frontier legend, "big government," and "big industry," the infringements of "railroad barons," "outsiders" and "bureaucrats." As with most all deeply embedded perspectives, this one had its justifications in certain circumstances and times and it still expresses an authentic focus on the prime scene, the local community.

However, a contrasting but no less common truism today is that the nation and world have changed radically under the impact of modern communications and transportation, that insular styles of yesteryear are no more, that the earth itself is fast becoming a "global village." Despite this generally recognized transition, the older thesis still continues, not just in upholding its basic values, but also, as found in this study, in befogging and confusing the actual relationships within the church.

Out of the inherited citizenry-versus-the-colossus mentality has grown a kind of schizoid image of the church, split between the intimate local congregation on the one side and the remote, impersonal denomination on the other. Sometimes, the implication almost has seemed to be that they are pitted against each other. This impression gained even greater prevalence in the financial squeeze on the churches recently at which time denominational officials talked of a new localism, a tendency to concentrate resources on the community level and downgrade the denomination. It also was registered in the catchphrases of the times, the "anti-institution" and "anti-establishment" temper among youths. While their main religious target was the local church rather than the denomination, the attitude contributed to the sense of cleavage, a "we" versus "they" syndrome.

A wide impression developed that the rupture especially afflicted the church. Some denominational leaders have come to feel that it characterizes a large proportion of the local clergy and laity, that the local people distrust and resent the denomination and are inclined to cut off support for it. "The superstructure as we now have it is going to topple like Solomon's Temple," a Chicago clergyman commented. "It appears that we are only important at the local level for the money that we can give the impersonal superstructure." Others, in their conversation, referred repeatedly to "us" as against "them."

Since this sort of rugged, scrappy independence has an honored place in the American legend, it sometimes is an almost instinctive reaction, staunch and handy to state. Considering this and other aspects of the contemporary climate that have magnified the idea of alienation between groups, the general supposition has

14

been that the attitude was rampant in the church, that there was a bitter "gap" between home and headquarters. But the findings don't support it. Rather, they show that for a strong majority, the opposite is true.

Most pastors and lay persons alike appreciate the denomination's importance to the congregation. Overall, 79 percent of them agreed or tended to agree with the statement, "The denomination is important to the local church." On the other hand, only 21 percent disagreed or tended to disagree, half of them merely "tending" to do so. But on the affirmative side, three-fourths of them "strongly agreed" or "agreed" that the denomination is vital to local church life, and only a fourth merely "tended" to do so. Clergy in the United States felt even more fully that the denomination is important, with those definitely disagreeing amounting to 2.5 percent.

"You're a part of total Lutheranism, not just small and separate," a San Francisco store owner commented. "You have to function as a whole."

Some felt less confident, but the supposition of a yawning hiatus, a "cold war" between the local scene and the denomination just didn't stack up. Denominational officials have worried and stewed about it and the casual expressions of it have convinced many local people that it exists, but as for their own feelings about it, most of them don't share it. It apparently has simply been blown up out of proportion to the facts. Clarifying the situation can contribute to more open, mutually aware communications, unencumbered by lurking misapprehensions and suspicions of disaffection. Instead of disenchantment, the great majority of the people feel that the local congregation importantly needs the denomination, that they are interdependent.

However, there also are other widespread assumptions about the denominations which find little concurrence among the membership. Chief among these is the idea that when the denomination's policy-making bodies, usually their representative conventions, take stands on controversial social issues, it irritates the rank-and-file members. The complaint is raised in almost every denominational assembly that the folks back home don't want it to meddle in economic, social or political concerns, that such actions weaken and divide the churches, create antagonism toward them and drive people out of them.

Here again, the impression is built up of a denomination in one category, the people apart in another, despite the elected, representative composition of denominational conventions. There also is ample, vocal evidence on the American scene of those who do resent denominational involvement in social problems. Numerous partisan organizations and factions have formed in recent years, specifically to oppose church efforts to apply its principles in the troublous sphere of social stresses and conflicts. These groups are quite articulate and lend broad credence to the supposition that the grassroots churchgoers, the heartland majority, object to denominational social pronouncements and church programs to enhance the status of racial minorities through open housing and better jobs.

Again, this is just not so for the bulk of American Christians. The study found that 88 percent of the clergy and 71 percent of the lay people in the United States feel their denominations should speak out on current social issues such as civil rights, the war and other pressing problems. They affirmed it as a responsibility, despite the organized campaigns against it, and even though it may, and often does, unsettle complacency and raise some hackles.

Sixty-eight percent of the clergy strongly agreed or agreed and 20 percent tended to agree it should be done, while 48 percent of the laity strongly agreed or agreed and another 23 percent tended to agree. Heavy majorities—more than 90 percent of the clergy and more than 70 percent of the laity also felt the denominations should support minority groups in obtaining open housing policies and upgraded employment in all parts of the nation.

Only on one question in this connection did a majority both of laity and clergy register disapproval. Sixty-one percent of the clergy and 76 percent of the laity disagreed or tended to disagree with denominations giving money to minority groups "with no strings attached." The phrase itself was purposely given a built-in bias that could be interpreted as inconsistent with the teaching of the Christian's responsibility for the use of his resources. In any case, while most rejected that approach, 39 percent of the clergy agreed with it or tended to do so, as did 24 percent of the laity.

Another denominational assumption, even more fancifully overrated, has a tinge of drama and costly courage about it. It holds that when a church does take a position on social concerns or supports daring, unconventional types of ministries or gives financial backing to minorities, a considerable number of church members are likely to withhold contributions. Some national leaders even gauge the effectiveness of their "mission" stance by the amount of negative feedback they get from the local churches, believing that the greater the resistance, the more effective the program. This resolute air of "damn-the-torpedoes, full speed ahead" is largely based on imagination. It may give some denominational leaders a sense of prophetic hardihood, but for

THE DENOMINATION AND SOCIAL ISSUES

table 1*

		strongly agree or agree	tend to agree	strongly disagree or disagree	tend to disagree
My denomination should support minority groups to secure open housing in all parts of the nation.	Clergy	77	14	3	6
	Laity	54	24	12	10
The church, especially my denomination, ought to speak out on social issues (such as civil rights) the war and the urban crisis.	Clergy	68	20	5	7
	Laity	48	23	17	12
My denomination should help minority groups secure more and better jobs.	Clergy	73	21	2	4
	Laity	51	24	13	12
My denomination should give minority groups more money with no strings attached.	Clergy	19	20	37	24
	Laity	11	13	52	24

* figures in percentages (Clergy N = 662 Laity N = 2785)

18

the most part, it does not derive from reality.

The actual reaction of church people was gauged in this question: "Have you withheld money from your church or denomination on account of any situation, issue, or program during the past year or two?" Ninety-four percent of the laity and 94 percent of the clergy said they have not done so. To resort to that technique, said a California Baptist, "is a form of boycott, penalizing the good parts of the program by withholding from others."

Among other comments: "We should give with trust." "The church administration is in the best position to know what the greatest needs are." "We generally hire people to responsible positions and they should be allowed to carry out their responsibilities." "We trust our headquarters."

Of the six percent of clergy and laity who have withheld contributions, their reasons for it generally did not correspond to those surmised among denominational officials. "Too much money was being spent on pleasing the people of the congregation and building a beautiful structure," a Minneapolis electrical engineer said in explaining his reduced giving. Another spurned an "unsatisfactory" appeal to buy a new organ. "Putting maintenance ahead of charity," complained another. An Indiana Methodist retaliated financially at a special youth program, saying it bordered "on blasphemy and sacrilege." Another said he had rebuffed a special collection because "I gave race relations money directly to the denomination. The local church singled out just one college to help. I wanted the money to go to all." Such explanations were typical.

The two most important reasons given for withholding money related to special appeals or programs which members didn't approve or to which they said they couldn't afford to contribute. It usually was some specifically immediate situation, with personal overtones, that spurred the monetary reprisal. Only one percent of the people—one out of 100—mentioned denominational support to minority groups as a reason for having shaved their gifts. Yet this is the area most prominently and regularly cited as causing a financial drain on the church. As measured by the data, it simply is not the case.

The suppositions live on, however, inspired by the heroic image of doing the right thing in the face of persecution and whatever the costs. But the findings indicate that this dauntless determination, however gutsy, is mostly battling windmills. The vast preponderance of members has not held back money because of any denominational innovation or activity, and in the case of the very few who have done so, their reasons usually were not the ones so often dramatized.

Unverified assumptions, however, are built as much on talk, perhaps more so, than on what people actually do. To explore this verbal dimension as a possible source of the general belief that church members strike back financially whenever the church deviates from their particular preferences, a different kind of question was asked to evoke what people say about it, apart from what they do. Here, the difference showed up strikingly. While only a tiny minority had actually done it, a good many more speculated that it could be justified.

The question: "Some people withhold money when the local church or denomination supports programs of which they disapprove. Do you think this is justified?"

While a majority said "no," the count was closer. The following table gives the breakdown. Most of those not in the definite "no" column gave a conditional response saying that it depends on the particular circumstances. However, a much larger percentage than had actually withheld money answered with an explicit "yes," that it could be justified. This still was only one in five lay persons and even fewer pastors, who theoretically considered such action defensible. They registered a latent, if not active, point of pocketbook revolt at some potential areas of church activity.

table 2*

IS WITHHOLDING JUSTIFIED?

		yes	no	depends
Clergy		14	58	28
Laity		22	52	25

* figures in percentages

Among their comments about what could justify a financial backlash: "Building too elaborately or embellishing the church more than is needed." "Handing money to minority groups with no strings attached." Making the church building into "an expensive, pretentious showplace." "Political programs adverse to New Testament teachings." Most of these people hadn't themselves withheld funds, but they do cite possibly catalyzing irritants, and they indicated a desire to keep the option open, perhaps for strategic leverage. Those who gave an indefinite answer took a somewhat similar tack, but usually on more fundamental grounds. Any decision to withhold money, one said, would depend on "whether or not it is put to a Christian use." It would depend, said another, "on the programs and how true they are to the Word of God and Bible teachings." These responses generally reflected an underlying recognition of the right of others to withhold support if they became convinced a program violated the teachings of the church or their own consciences.

The majority, which matched what they said with what they have done, expressed a church commitment unqualified by personal differences over specific programs. "If you are going to support something, you either do it or don't," one observed. "It's not based on whether you agree or disagree." Another said, "Loyalty demands support." "The only justification for withholding funds is lack of ability to contribute." You don't stalk off in a huff, they were saying, just because you didn't get your way in how your congregation decides to go about its business.

There were extensive indications that lay members and pastors often know little about denominational programs or the rationale behind them. In this situation, the degree of trust in denominational leaders appears quite high. A question in this category also brought out that when it comes to specific undertakings, individual reservations about them are not considered sufficient cause for refusing support. The test question read:

"A person should support a church only so long as it supports activities he agrees with."

Only three percent of the clergy and nine percent of the laity in the United States decisively concurred with that personally restrictive vision of the church's responsibilities. Others who tended to concur with it brought the total in the affirmative classification to seven percent of the clergy and 16 percent of the laity. But the overwhelming majority—93 percent of the clergy and 84 percent of the laity—definitely reject or tend to reject supporting the church only so long as it adheres to their own particular leanings.

"If the church has to agree with me and all the other members, we would never get anything done," observed a burly San Francisco dock superintendent. Others commented, "One opinion is not sufficient to evaluate what is worthwhile." Another put it even more bluntly, "I can disagree with something and still it's good." The findings make a conspicuous point: That the down-home "middle America" Christians are not nearly as narrow as sociological analysts generally portray them.

Furthermore, this more knowledgeable, savvy church membership wants a greater voice in determining how both the local congregations and the denominations use their resources. Most of them feel that the only way they can get it is by "earmarking" their offerings for special purposes. Half of the laity think this ought to be the standard, but only 30 percent of them say it now is being done. "If people know where the money is going, they would be more inclined to give more," one put it. And another, "The church thus expresses its specific concerns." "Unless we designate it," another said, "the gift becomes lost in the large work of the church." A fourth of the members aren't interested in it, however, expressing confidence that denominational leaders can more reliably decide where the needs are keenest. One noted, "They know the needs better than the local church."

THE PASTOR AS INTERMEDIARY

The local pastor is the relay point, the interagent, between the congregation and the denomination in the church's operational structure. He is the liaison man through whom the members convey their opinions, ideas and concerns to the denomination, and through whom the denomination passes its information and advice to the congregations.

And here, this study suggests, resides a bottleneck.

The data show that the clergy and laity have differing perspectives of the church and since the clergy views are those most often heard by denominational leaders, the extent to which a pastor registers his own rather than his congregation's feelings adds to the prevailing denominational misconceptions of their constituencies. The same roadblock can operate the other way.

But just how different are the pastors' perceptions and what sort of information do they fail to pass on?

For one thing, clergy are more interested than lay people in the denomination's responsibility for promoting non-local ministries and involvement in social issues. Some of this difference can be directly attributed to the laity's lack of knowledge about the denomination, a lack that the clergy has failed to fill. On the other hand, the message is clear that the laity want some help from the denomination in dealing with current problems and situations in the local church. But the clergy, by and large, are not registering that need nor transmitting the help that is available since they are unaware that it is wanted. Thus the effectiveness of the denomination is stymied because the intermediary is not letting some of the signals through from either direction.

On a matter in which the signals did come through strongly, as in the misapprehension that lay people often withhold funds out of disagreement with denominational programs, distortion took place in the transmission process. The implication is that the clergy sometimes project their own fears and feelings on lay members, and to the extent that they do, they inhibit rather than facilitate communications within the denomination.

Figures already cited show that just as many clergy as laity have withheld money from the church, undercutting the presumption that this is mainly a lay tactic. Beyond this, however, some pronounced differences between clergy and laity emerged through a question put only to those who felt such action could be justified.

Notably, the percentage of pastors prone to withhold contributions because of minority demands is about double that of lay people. A considerably larger proportion of clergy also cites doctrinal reasons, suggesting a tendency to clothe opposition to social involvement in theology. On the other hand, more than twice as big

table 3*

MOST IMPORTANT THINGS DENOMINATION SHOULD DO FOR A LOCAL CHURCH

Could you tell me some situations, programs, or issues that you would consider serious enough to cause people to withhold money?

	Clergy	Laity
no response	12.7	27.6
doctrinal	19	11.6
building	2.5	3.7
non-gospel activity	3.8	5.9
support minority demands	30.3	15.9
social involvement	11.4	15.9
war, draft-dodgers	3.8	4.5
way money is used by denomination	11.4	8.6
other	5.1	6.3

* This table includes 79 clergy and 510 laity of the United States, those saying withholding could be justified. Figures in percentages.

a percentage of laity avoided specifying any particular reasons, basing the justification for possibly withholding money merely on the contention that the option should be kept open in case of sufficient, though presently undiscerned, cause.

The data show that clergy to a greater degree than lay people have in mind particular gripes against the denomination—a total of nearly 90 percent of them, compared to about 70 percent of the laity. Among potential incitements to reprisal cited by one group or the other: "Church politics." "Too much overhead." "Programs on police brutality, welfare and migrants." "Emphasis on property over people." "Undemocratic way of setting giving." "Programs not teaching of the church." "Dislike minister." "Special funds for minorities." "Don't agree with foreign missions." "People should have the right to designate."

The higher degree of specified negativism in the clergy suggest that they, the intermediaries, may be at the roots of some of the general misimpressions. That some specific information is not getting through to the laity was brought out in this question about supporting the church: "Have you seen any literature about stewardship within the past year?" Ninety-eight percent of the clergy had seen some, indicating an ample flow of material from denominations down to the pastors. However, only 61 percent of the laity reported ever seeing any such material. Somewhere between the national denominational offices and the local lay people, the information had been filtered out. The key man in this screening process is the local pastor who receives the material and decides whether or not to pass it down. Often, the findings show, the decision is not to do so.

This is a critical point in the church informational channels. The data show that if the laity receive the literature, they either read it thoroughly (48 percent of them) or skim through it (another 49 percent). Only three percent fail to do either. To the extent the clergy decide not to let the laity have the materials, they intervene to clog the denominational process, rather than carrying out their part in it.

Another potential obstacle is the denominational staff member who makes judgments about which programs to pass on to the local clergymen. Separated from the local situation, he has about the same difficulties in understanding it as the local clergyman seems to have in understanding the laity. This means there are two circuit points—the staff member at the denominational level and the pastor at the local level— either of whom can block the flow of interpretative materials to the laity. In order both for the lay people to understand denominational efforts and for denominational leaders to understand the local laity's concerns, the facts must pass through agents at both levels. Both undoubtedly tend to select the emphases that suit them, filter out others. In cases where clergy requests are made to the denomination for special assistance, information deemed unpalatable may be omitted. At the same time, the study shows, some information from the denomination for the laity obviously is not getting past the clergy.

THE AVERAGE CONGREGATION

Despite the many denominational assumptions about the "average" congregation, there simply is no such thing. This study brought out the diversity and boundless variety of local parishes and people in them, rather than their similarity or standardized norms. None could be basically equated with another. People's personal experiences, their families, their special problems and backgrounds, their expectations, plans for the future, their particular towns and regions, their social positions, ages, education, income level and a myriad of other factors distinguish individuals and groups from one another.

The sundry factors can be classified and collated to arrive at an "average" member but the average is only a computed type, not a real person. Similarly, congregational factors can be placed in categories to establish an "average" congregation, but it, too, is simply a statistic.

Sometimes such grouping is considered necessary and there are various common factors that can be used to do it. For instance, in this study, classification by age indicated that 26 percent of the members are between 50 and 64 years old, 22 percent between 40 and 49, another 17 percent between 30 and 39, but only nine percent between 20 and 29 and only seven percent in their teens. The data also revealed that pastors in the United States tend to be younger than Canadian pastors.

These figures, however, like other factors of income, education and sex, differ from place to place and from one size of church to another, making the averages mostly meaningless. The implication here is that church program creators and curriculum writers need to stop thinking in terms of the "average" or typical congregation and stop producing materials for it. Material should be offered for its intrinsic worth, not out of any statistically projected typecasting of congregations. This myth of a typical congregation needs to be put to rest, and a new approach to church programing developed.

Numerous other assumptions were found in the study to be untenable, but at this point, only a preliminary sketch is offered of some of them.

In the present era of theological ferment and diversity, it has been widely maintained that classical Christian doctrine must be reinterpreted in accord with an age of technology and modern modes of thought to make it intelligible. Many scholars contend that the traditional formulations fail to illuminate or convince people today and must be recast in new perspective more in line with present-day knowledge and made more directly relevant to contemporary problems and concerns. They say this is necessary because of a more highly educated population and especially for sophisticated youth and young adults. To stick to the cultural and religious symbols of another era, they conclude, is to relegate religion to a quaint, archaic past and escape its pressing truths.

To support this thesis, they cite various statistical trends suggesting that institutional religion, as presently perceived, is not acceptable to coming generations. Many people, with a certain melancholy, tend to become convinced that the analysts are right, that this is, indeed, a "post-Christian" era, that the old message just doesn't ring true and hit home to late twentieth century minds. This bleak mood affects both clergy and laity and drains the spirit of the whole church, echoing in such phrases as "crisis of faith" and "crisis of belief."

But is it, basically, true? Is this a "post-Christian" age?

The data in this study show that people, of all ages and categories, of much education and little, young and old, at upper economic levels and low, strongly subscribe to the classically stated doctrines of Christianity, the concepts that the theologians say urgently need updating. These include belief in God as heavenly Father who watches over each person and to whom each is accountable, in salvation from sin, in the Scriptures as the Word of God, in Jesus Christ as God's revelation to man, in Christ as a continuing living reality and in eternal life beyond death. These are the central, traditional affirmations of the church and they are not counted odd or outmoded by Americans, even by those only marginally associated with the church, but rather, are overwhelmingly believed.

Whether modern preaching reflects it is another question.

THE WORK OF THE LOCAL CHURCH

A powerful and pervasive assumption that has been built up by sociological critics is that the local church serves mainly as a "social club" whose members expect it to function like one, providing compatible friendships, pleasant activity and a safe, respectable environment for youngsters, having little to do with sin, sinners and the unclean. The supposition has it that the church should cater to its members' tastes and personal needs, but stay out of general community conflicts and stresses, lest these controversial matters disrupt the church's social harmony and drive members to desert it.

This belittling image of the local church hit its high water mark in the fifties and sixties. It still has considerable vocal support, and as with most popular assumptions, it can be argued with one-sided, indirect evidence. Most people do regard the church as a personal center of comfort, reassurance and refuge, but they clearly do not so delimit it in the narrow fashion that has been portrayed, nor even rate that purpose among the prime objectives.

As found in this study, the paramount No. 1 task of the local church is reaching beyond itself in evangelism—"winning others to Christ." This emphasis is considerably stronger in the United States than in Canada, reflecting historical differences in the religious development in the two countries. Other highly rated responsibilities of the local church were to provide religious instruction, worship, the sacraments, ministerial services and to help the needy. Selected next, midway in a list of 14 possible functions, were to "serve as social conscience to the community" and "support overseas missions." Lower down, in the bottom half of the list, came such subsidiary items as providing "fellowship" and "facilities for activities" of members. The "social club" canard just didn't wash.

"People meet others in all walks of life and don't need the church for this," went a typical comment. "The church should be for religion, not socializing."

At the same time, in the midway categories, noticeable differences showed up. Clergy in the United States ranked the church's duty to serve as "social conscience to the community" in sixth place, while laity ranked it eighth. In Canada, clergy ranked it fourth, while laity ranked it sixth. Simply put, lay people do not see quite as strongly as clergy the need for the local church to act as a corporate "conscience" in their communities, but they do give it middling value.

This, and other functions that were ranked low on the local scale, such as to "influence legislation" and "support minority groups" or to "build low-cost housing," may appear to contradict the laity's general acceptance of the denomination's duty to act and speak in the social sphere. However, the explanation seems to be that lay people see a distinction in types of responsibilities with some tasks beyond local capabilities. Said the wife of an insurance man, "Other organizations are doing this type of work."

Furthermore, lay people are particularly aware of differences among themselves when it comes to ethical concerns in the local community. The denomination, less personal than the local church and more removed from the immediate pressures, is not so subject to these constraints and can act more freely on principle.

Generally, members feel that the local church, being dependent on the local community for support and members, must remain a bulwark of personal values and teachings, and be wary of entanglements in divisive local issues. Yet they're willing for the wider institution to take on these problems. In their view, each has its work which it can do, and in a complex world of diverse influences and abilities, for one to presume it can duplicate the other could be not only unproductive but foolhardy. They seem to espouse, not a contradiction, but a kind of hard-headed realism, a combined pragmatism and idealism, reflecting, perhaps, an old dictum of Jesus: "Be as wise as serpents and innocent as doves."

In any case, the continual academic exhortations to the local church to take a more assertive role in community affairs as a corporate "conscience" and aggressive activist has fallen largely on deaf ears. At least it hasn't convinced the bulk of the American Christian constituency, which considers the local church primarily as the maker and molder of conscience, and not its muscle, nor the point for flexing it.

WHY PEOPLE LOSE INTEREST

The same viewpoint was substantiated through inquiries into why some people lose interest in the church. Clergymen perpetuate an idea that apathy and dropouts result from the church having become unimportant in modern society. Both in the United States and Canada, clergymen see this as the main cause of people losing interest. But in neither country do lay people buy that line at all. They put it down as a seventh-rate factor, compared to the clergy's estimate of it as No. 1. However, while the laity consider the church important, they imply that the clergy's version of it is not their kind of church and that what turns people off is not the church's unimportance, but the pressure of time and other more compelling interests.

"My church activities have moved more into the area where I do my everyday work," one man put it. "Nothing to do with my faith has changed, but it's just that I feel the place I should be working is outside the church. My own faith has moved out of the church and into the secular world. I feel I teach Sunday school all the time in work."

Lay people say that because the church functions in a diversified society of many beneficial causes that compete for everyone's time, the church must meet the needs of members for growth and service if it is to keep them interested and involved. As for the main reasons why interest sags, they cited lack of time and getting absorbed in nonchurch organizations, which are two sides of the same coin. Coupled with it, in third place, they blamed dislike for the pastor.

Next in line, they listed loss of confidence in the church and its failure to offer an appealing program, meaning that it was not meeting their personal needs for dealing with the problems of life and so inclining them to invest their available time and energies elsewhere.

Although the tritely repeated assumption has

been that the church's "social involvement" or lack of it alienates members—in the first case because they want a quiet, comforting sanctuary and in the second case because they want decisive, relevant action—neither factor figured significantly as causes of disenchantment in the minds of the people. In fact, they discounted both, ranking them near the bottom in a list of 16 possibilities. However, U. S. clergymen ranked church "social involvement" in the upper-half bracket of causes for alienation, again indicating that they inflate the risks of such activity and are more worried about its effects than are ordinary churchgoers.

While the lay people want a church that deals first and foremost with definitive proclamation of the faith, its extension and their nurture in it, they're not as uptight as the clergy about "social involvement" if there is time and money left for it. On the other hand, the clergy are more prone to assert they favor it, even though they're far more uneasy about its negative effects than the members are themselves.

In short, it's a matter of priorities. The people don't want involvement with social concerns to detract from forthright cultivation of the Gospel and its application to personal growth and orientation in life. In this comparative sense, the clergy are partially right. But according to the data, they have the situation somewhat backward. It's the inadequacy of dealing with the first concern that chiefly turns people off, and not, as the clergy tend to imagine, dealing with the second.

REASONS FOR GIVING

Theories and surmises abound about why people give to the church and other philanthropic causes range from habit, social pressure and getting a sense of satisfaction out of it, to fear and guilt. These influences may figure remotely on some substrata, but on the level of conscious awareness, they hardly count at all. When people were asked to choose six reasons for giving from a list of 16 possibilities, including the commonly asserted motives of feeling guilty if they don't give, fearing God's judgment, social pressure of friends and associates, habit or because they feel good about it, none of these even made the top ten. They were discounted.

But the most frequently cited reasons did have a clearly personal base, rather than pointing beyond it to external accomplishment. "Gratitude to God" was easily the main reason for giving, followed by convictions that it is a "part of worship," a "privilege to share," out of "love for others," or as an "obligation placed on man by God." These possibilities also had been anticipated, since the list included them, but the theological phrasing leaves room for some nuances, which show up in other portions of the study.

These have to do particularly with the heavy impact of employment, size of income and how much of it is left over after family needs are met. Any of these can weigh on giving to the church, and are among the main reasons cited for not giving at all. Furthermore, while reasons for giving are most often couched in theological terms, actual reasons may be pragmatic. For example, the "gratitude to God" impulse sometimes was elaborated in such comments as "Thank God I'm better off than a lot of people."

Nevertheless, whether in comparison to others or not, people affirm that their giving arises out of gratitude as a part of worshiping God and from a sense of duty toward the church and others. However, lay people give considerably less

35

than clergy, who display much greater consistency in their identifying serving God with the giving of their material resources, since they actually do more of it. While lay people also equate worshiping God with giving, other phases of the study showed many of them actually give almost nothing in the course of a year.

In this tangible sense, the genuinely decisive motivations appear to vary from those affirmed —a normal condition in many areas of life. Aside from clinical probing, it simply is impossible to tell exactly why people do things. All that really can be determined is when, how and how often they do things. In this sense, the truly controlling motives can be determined only by observable behavior. Yet an individual's behavior is conditioned by the group, by its norms of conduct and expectations and by those within it whose respect he values. All of these influences must be considered in assessing motives, and since the family usually is the primary group and context out of which a person acts, its situation, needs, desires and demands bear strongly on motives in other spheres, including the church.

It thus comes as no surprise that the major influence affecting the amount of money given to the church is plain practicality—the size of income. Balancing this on the altruistic side, however, the "needs of the church" are the second biggest influence on how much is given. When it comes to reasons for not giving at all, however, family situations predominate. The main reasons cited are to concentrate on providing the family with "the good things of life" or to meet extra family expenses for such things as schooling, illness or caring for parents. These concerns emerged as the primary conditioners regulating the flow of support to the church.

Other clues turned up in the study indicated

there are not just one audience, but several "audiences" in the church, each responding to differing stimuli and means of communication. Among the factors that delineate these distinctive groups or "audiences" are age, the degree of commitment to the institution and the position held in it, as well as educational level, family income and length of residence in the community. None of these by itself is a sure index of attitudes about the church or how much support is given it. But several of them combined ordinarily indicate the behavior that can be expected in regard to the church.

For example, as found in this study, young adults generally are better educated than older adults and tend to look on support of the church in rational rather than emotional terms. They also generally have obligations to children, a stage of responsibility past for those over 50. The older members also reflect a greater need for stability in the teachings of the church than do younger members. These varying combinations, along with others, affect feelings toward the church and the extent to which it is supported.

In concrete terms, however, each "audience" gives to the church according to what they have available. Motives? Who can really say? They're a nebulous mixture of commitment, involvement, gratitude for life, appreciation for good fortune and health, interacting with expectations of family and friends. Out of this miscellany, seasoned with strongly affirmed devotion to God's purposes, grow the decisions about giving to the church and working in it.

THE FUTURE OF THE CHURCH

A recurring modern shibboleth is that the church is dying. It has been said before in nearly every age, but its current repetition, abetted by ceaseless polls heralding collapse in mere transient downtrends without the balancing parallels and sharper ebbs of history, strike a melancholy mood among Christians. The doom-sayers have had a heydey, declaring that the church is outmoded, an archaic vestige of another day, decaying and plunging toward its demise. That's a dirge that has throbbed around the church throughout its life and which mocked its very beginnings. Always, as now, the church faced difficulties, challenges, internal problems and acute need for renewal and confidence.

But however religiously depressing the modern atmosphere may be, most church people today are neither resigned to it, nor persuaded by it. Out of some elemental awareness drawn from faith itself, they reject the gloomy presumptions and dire forecasts of downfall. A strong majority believe that the church will be just as important or more important a decade hence. "The church has been asleep for a long time, but it's waking up," said a Halifax lawyer. Whether of intuition or believing hope, or out of whatever motives, in contrast to the prevailing pessimism of the day about the church, most people see its road as up, not down. And they should know, for they are that of which they speak, its innards, its energies, its perseverance and its dedication, the stuff of which it is made. They are the church.

But a crucial influence on which way it moves is how alert and responsive it is to realities within itself, how sharply it discerns its own inner distortions and mistaken presumptions, how readily it balances and rectifies them. Old mind-sets, the entrenched assumptions, are a hardy breed. They become almost instinctive, like the ways of the labrador duck. This creature, a native of swampy ground, to get its food pressed down with its broad webbed feet to force up worms. Even when born and reared in captivity and living in a zoo, it still pressed down with its webbed feet at eating time on the unyielding concrete floor. Some of the misassumptions in the church are as resistant as that concrete. They've been around a long time, a cause of frustrations and bafflement, the familiar modus operandi. But according to the pointers of this study, continuing to press down with those webbed feet in the familiar gesture just won't feed the flock.

2.

the core and
its consequences

"I believe in God, the Father almighty, creator of heaven and earth, and in Jesus Christ his only Son, our Lord . . . I believe in the Holy Spirit, the holy catholic church . . . the forgiveness of sins, the resurrection of the body, and the life everlasting."

These affirmations in the Apostles' Creed are the bedrock beliefs of Christianity. They took form in the shadowy early centuries of the faith and served as its guarding standard in a surrounding sea of paganism. They carried the cause through persecution, dispersions, state intrigues, internal struggles, deviations, dark ages and schism. They spanned the break between eastern and western Christendom and later between Protestantism and Roman Catholicism, forging a continuous bond among the various followers of Christ. They stood as the common heritage, the ramparts against assault, past and present, the cement of the entire church.

But do they still stand? Are they still believed?

To judge by some of the religious laments of the day, by some of the surgical dissections and dismal diagnoses of the church, by the "word games" of biblical linguistic analysts, by the popularized and often misrepresented "demythologizers," by the findings of numerous surveys conditioned by technical or regional limitations, by the theological diversity in academic circles whose pursuit of "new" interpretations has included "new" advocacy of the old conclusion that "God is dead," you would think—judging by all these unsettling tendencies—that the ancient Christian convictions have just about had it, that they're passé, a withering relic.

You might even get that impression by listening to the hesitant modern sermons that sometimes tend to apologize for the transworldly aspects of the faith and to qualify it with present "knowns" and its utilitarian relevance rather than to assert it fully and freely. The question comes back in reference to the clergy, too: Do they really believe it? Are their convictions slipping, or are they merely being tactful to try to keep in touch with the educated "secular" mind, so as to hold its interest and subtly point it beyond the immediately demonstrable truths without directly saying so?

Both questions—whether American church people still subscribe to the founding and perpetuating core convictions of their faith and whether the modern clergy, products of advanced biblical scholarship and untrammeled theological inquiry, still believe the basic propositions—were explored in this study. The answer, briefly, is that they do, both groups of them, in the United States and Canada. And they do so overwhelmingly.

The study, using carefully developed methods for measuring representatively the full spectrum of Protestant population in both countries, found that American church people and their clergy, rather than retreating from the strange, hopeful concepts that grew out of Judaism and the life of Jesus, strongly and definitely believe them,

41

whether they talk easily about them or not. They may be reticent about the more mysterious elements in sitting-room conversation and even in the pulpit, but when it comes to their private reflection, they hold the old tenets true.

The general impression has been that modern America has gone downhill religiously, that in the simpler, earthier past of the continent's settlement by Europeans and into the early part of this century, we were a thoroughly religious people, dedicated to the church and its underlying convictions, but nowadays thought and culture have become secular, ideas and people put on the computer and all nature robbed of its sacred character by science and manipulation. Actually, the available statistics of prior years don't accommodate this nostalgic image of a devout past.

What data there are indicate that the proportion of the population belonging to the churches was quite small in the frontier period and that it gradually has increased through the years, despite temporary drops, reaching its highest percentage in modern times. Yet this yardstick, affected by the vagaries and methodological differences in accumulating statistics, also is uncertain. The variables of categorizing and completeness make comparisons unreliable. The general, consistent indications, however, are that throughout history, the proportion of people wholeheartedly committed to the Christian faith has been relatively small, however much their influence on their times may become apparent to later historians.

Moreover, while those effectively committed may be relatively few, beliefs may be held extensively in a passive way. The question then becomes not just what people believe, but what it means to them and what they do about it.

In this study, attitudes were measured in three categories, namely: the extent to which American church people affirm the traditional basic concepts of Christianity, the kind of expectations and needs they find filled in the church, and thirdly, the manner in which they put their beliefs into practice.

The test statements used in examining what people believe are broad in scope, but they cover the main, historic framework of the faith and were applied to determine the degree to which they are accepted or rejected. To avoid confronting people with familiar terminology that might evoke preconditioned, unthinking responses, the phraseology was modified from that of the ancient creeds, but was designed to convey the same meanings. People were asked to state whether they strongly agreed, agreed, tended to agree, tended to disagree, disagreed or strongly disagreed, thus gauging the intensity of belief. The results, simplified by grouping together the positive and negative categories, are shown in Table 4 on page 44.

The mean scores, reflecting the intensity of responses, are shown in Table 5, page 45. Based on a rating system ranging from one for "strongly agree" to six for "strongly disagree," the lower the score, the stronger the agreement. Any score up to 3.5 is in the agree range.

All of the basic premises were heavily affirmed —belief in a personal God to whom individuals are accountable, in God's revelation in Jesus Christ, in eternal life, in Christ as a present living reality, in the revelation of God's Word in Scriptures, in salvation from sin and in the teachings of the church. While these concepts were supported by an average 98 percent of the

table 4*

REACTIONS TO BELIEF STATEMENTS

	U.S. Clergy		United Church of Canada Clergy		U.S. Laity		United Church of Canada Laity	
	positive	negative	positive	negative	positive	negative	positive	negative
I believe in God as a heavenly Father, who watches over me and to whom I am accountable.	97.3	2.7	93.9	6.1	97.8	2.2	90.6	9.4
I believe that God revealed Himself to man in Jesus Christ.	99.8	.2	100	0	99	1	93.4	6.6
I believe in eternal life.	99.1	.9	100	0	97.3	2.7	79.8	20.2
I believe that Christ is a living reality.	99.8	.2	100	0	97.6	2.4	84.6	15.4
I believe that the Word of God is revealed in the Scriptures.	99.1	.9	97	3	98.4	1.6	91.4	8.6
I believe in salvation as release from sin and freedom for a new life with God.	96.5	3.5	94.9	5.1	96.8	3.2	81.2	18.8
I believe honestly and wholeheartedly in the doctrines and teachings of the church.	95.5	4.5	95	5	96.4	3.6	87.2	12.8

• figures in percentages (U.S. Clergy N = 564   Laity N = 2344; Canada Clergy N = 98   Laity N = 441)

REACTION TO BELIEF STATEMENTS

table 5*

	Clergy		Laity	
	United States	United Church, Canada	United States	United Church, Canada
I believe in God as a Heavenly Father who watches over me and to whom I am accountable.	1.51	1.97	1.42	2.05
I believe that God revealed Himself to man in Jesus Christ.	1.19	1.31	1.44	1.84
I believe in eternal life.	1.35	1.61	1.50	2.27
I believe that Christ is a living reality.	1.22	1.44	1.55	2.26
I believe that the word of God is revealed in the Scriptures.	1.45	1.90	1.57	2.10
I believe in salvation as release from sin and freedom for new life with God.	1.61	2.03	1.72	2.51
I believe honestly and wholeheartedly in the doctrines and teachings of the Church.	1.71	2.13	1.74	2.30

* Based on a scale of 1 to 6. 1 = strongly agree; 2 = agree; 3 = tend to agree; 4 = tend to disagree; 5 = disagree; 6 = strongly disagree.

clergy and an average 97 percent of the laity in the United States and by an average 97 percent of the Canadian clergy, the Canadian lay people are not quite so unanimous on some points. An average 87 percent of them supported the concepts, but even this large majority still is considerably less than that of their own pastors and less than that of the clergy and laity in the United States. The difference was evident in regard to each of the test statements, but was least pronounced in regard to belief in Jesus as God's revelation to man. Here the near unanimity went across the board.

Despite the broad pattern of concurrence in this doctrinal phase of the inquiry, there are clear, though minor, differences between clergy and lay people. In both countries, the clergy are most overwhelmingly persuaded of Christ's revelation of God, his living presence and eternal life. In slight contrast, U. S. lay people registered their strongest beliefs in Jesus as God's revelation to man, in a personal God demanding individual accountability and in eternal life. In somewhat greater contrast, Canadian laity displayed their keenest beliefs in Jesus as God's revelation, in God demanding individual accountability and in Scripture. Only 80 percent of the Canadian laity expressed belief in eternal life, compared to close to 100 percent of the clergy in both countries and the U. S. laity who did so, either strongly agreeing, agreeing, or tending to agree with it.

Notably, the test statement evoking the least fervor of belief had to do with the ecclesiastical presentation of faith—the "doctrines and teachings of the church." Comparatively, it got the lowest mean score among clergy in both countries and among U. S. laity. Canadian lay people, again displaying their difference, rated it next to last, putting in last place belief in "release from sin." This was rated next-to-last by clergy and by U. S. laity.

However, what brings down the rankings for both items, particularly in the United States, lies primarily in the varying emphases by the different denominations. In some denominations, church "doctrines and teachings" are rated about as high as the more directly personal statements of belief, while in other denominations, not so much enthusiasm is registered for the official interpretations.

Nevertheless, the degree of commitment to all of these propositions is remarkably high, strongly within the "agree" range. Yet the results do indicate fine lines of distinction, and when these occur between clergy and the laity, they can cause strains in the church. Since the clergy generally determine the directions and educative vitality of the church, the differences, left unconfronted and unreconciled, can affect the support of the people for it.

The minor differences, however, do not show up only between clergy and laity, but also among lay members, according to various classifications. One conditioner is their age. The differing degrees of commitment, according to age, is shown in Table 6 on page 48.

Only with two of the test statements is the extent of agreement about the same for all age categories of clergy and laity—the beliefs that God "revealed Himself to man in Jesus Christ" and in Christ as "a living reality." The agreement with the other five statements varies somewhat according to rôle or age category.

However, lay people in all age categories, from teen-agers to those over 65, are quite in accord about their belief in eternal life. Surprisingly, the younger people affirm it just as

table 6*

REACTIONS TO BELIEF STATEMENTS BY AGE

	Clergy					Laity					
	20-29	30-39	40-49	50-64	65+	14-19	20-29	30-39	40-49	50-64	65+
I believe in God as a Heavenly Father who watches over me and to whom I am accountable.	1.89	1.59	1.51	1.42	1.37	1.71	1.49	1.40	1.41	1.41	1.34
I believe that God revealed Himself to man in Jesus Christ.	1.26	1.18	1.21	1.17	1.27	1.70	1.45	1.38	1.41	1.44	1.46
I believe in eternal life.	1.59	1.38	1.39	1.28	1.22	1.51	1.50	1.51	1.49	1.48	1.51
I believe that Christ is a living reality.	1.19	1.23	1.26	1.19	1.24	1.86	1.57	1.58	1.55	1.54	1.50
I believe that the word of God is revealed in the Scriptures.	1.48	1.39	1.51	1.43	1.63	1.83	1.63	1.57	1.54	1.55	1.50
I believe in salvation as release from sin and freedom for a new life with God.	1.85	1.56	1.54		1.59	1.90	1.85	1.74	1.69		1.62
I believe honestly and wholeheartedly in the doctrines and teachings of the Church.	1.85	1.78	1.79	1.65	1.41	2.16	1.90	1.80	1.74	1.33	1.53

* Based on a scale of 1 to 6. 1 = strongly agree; 2 = agree; 3 = tend to agree; 4 = tend to disagree; 5 = disagree; 6 = strongly disagree. The lower the score, the stronger the agreement. U.S. only.

strongly as the older lay people, and more strongly than do clergymen under 30. Yet they, too, embrace it quite heartily. Among the clergy, it is most strongly upheld by the most experienced and mature. Overall, despite marginal variations, the Easter promise of a future life beyond death is supported with an overwhelming intensity by church people today.

In other respects, both the younger clergy and laity reflect some rather mutually distinguishing marks. Generally they're least concerned about official church doctrines, release from sin and the concept of God as a Father demanding accountability, while the older clergy and laity generally are more committed to those beliefs. The inclination of the older people suggests, in a sense, a relatively more passive view of the church as a protector and dispenser of a "packaged" system of salvation handed on from generation to generation, while the lesser concern for those points among younger people and their keener concern for Christ as a present "living reality" suggests a more active, mobile view of God's work in the world.

These shadings in perspective can underlie tensions in the local churches as well as in the denomination. The implication also is that the balance of emphasis in style of churchmanship may be undergoing a change among clergy and laity under 50. But this does not imply any lessening of belief, only a varying tendency about how that belief is expressed among men.

Interestingly, the Scriptures are consistently affirmed as revealing the Word of God, but least so among teen-agers. Making for a case of strange bedfellows, these youngsters among the laity and the aging pastors over 65 among the clergy are curiously similar in registering less thorough-going confidence in Scriptures than do the others in their groups. On the whole, however, the clergy, those who generally have the most background, understanding and training in biblical scholarship, express the greatest degree of certitude that the Bible conveys God's Word. The adult laity also does so, but simply with less sweeping certainty.

Throughout the age breakdown, the teenagers between 14 and 19 generally display the most traces of skepticism. They agree, but aren't inclined to do it so strongly. Among all others, these youngsters are least supportive of ecclesiastically defined "doctrines and teachings." Although agreeing, they barely do so. They're also less supportive of other concepts, except eternal life. However, these inklings of a "generation gap" don't last discernibly; they pass. Above the age of 20, the differences between age groups swiftly fade, merge and blend. In regard to central beliefs, aside from churchly style, there does not appear to be a deep or continuing gap between older and younger lay people, despite the hand-wringing about it.

VALUES OF CHURCH LIFE

The second set of test statements sought to determine what needs people find filled in the church and what benefits they draw from it. Somewhat disturbingly, they are not as fully convinced that the church supplies the various personal reinforcements as they are of the basic beliefs. Somewhere between the ideal and the realization falls a thin shadow. But perhaps this is inevitable, a reflection of the universal disparity between human aspiration and human competence. Despite this, however, the great majority finds elemental needs met within the church community. Responses to the test statements are shown in percentages in Table 7, page 52, with those strongly agreeing, agreeing or tending to agree grouped under "positive" and those tending to disagree, disagreeing or strongly disagreeing grouped under "negative."

For greater precision, the mean scores also are shown, in Table 8, page 53. These reflect keenness of agreement or disagreement, scored on a basis of one for "strongly agree" to six for "strongly disagree," with the other four levels in between. The lower the score, the stronger the affirmation, with anything up to 3.5 in the "agree" range.

The most overwhelmingly cited sustenance derived from the church for U. S. laity and clergy and for Canadian clergy is the "strength and courage for dealing with the trials and problems of life." This represents a broadly inclusive view of the church, conceiving of its resources as directly applicable to the issues of everyday living and not just confined to the sanctuary. By a thin margin, Canadian laity rated this broad function second, focusing slightly more on the church as a shielding "comfort and refuge from the trials and problems of life." U. S. laity put this insular value second, giving priority—as did the clergy—to the more comprehensive view that the church girds people for the rough-and-tumble challenges of living in the world.

However, two clear differences were evident between the clergy and laity in both countries. For one thing, the laity is much less inclined to equate financial support of the church with a sense of closeness to God. Both in Canada and the United States, they rate this corollary fourth, or last in significance, among the various factors. In contrast, clergy in both countries rate it second, suggesting that they are more keenly conscious of the deeply interwoven, interacting links

table 7*

EXPECTATIONS OF THE CHURCH

	U.S. Clergy		United Church of Canada Clergy		U.S. Laity		United Church of Canada Laity	
	positive	negative	positive	negative	positive	negative	positive	negative
The church is important to me as a place where I get strength and courage for dealing with the trials and problems of life.	97.2	2.8	95	5	94.3	5.7	82.7	17.3
Church is important as a place to go for comfort and refuge from the trials and problems of life.	81.9	18.1	69.5	31.5	92.2	7.8	85.4	14.6
Church membership has helped me to meet the right kind of people.	78.3	21.7	55.4	44.6	82.3	17.6	65.7	34.3
The more I support the church financially, the closer I feel to it and to God.	89.6	10.4	74.6	25.4	69.2	30.8	39.6	61.4

* figures in percentages

table 8*

EXPECTATIONS OF THE CHURCH BY CLERGY AND LAITY

	Clergy		Laity	
	U.S.	U.C.C.	U.S.	U.C.C.
The Church is important to me as a place where I get strength and courage for dealing with the trials and problems of life.	1.68	1.96	1.84	2.46
Church is important as a place to go for comfort and refuge from the trials and problems of life.	2.80	2.95	1.99	2.39
Church membership has helped me to meet the right kinds of people.	2.62	3.29	2.44	3.01
The more I support the Church financially, the closer I feel to it and to God.	2.16	2.69	2.80	3.81

* The lower the score, the stronger agreement, based on a scale of 1 to 6. 1 = strongly agree; 2 = agree; 3 = tend to agree; 4 = tend to disagree; 5 = disagree; 6 = strongly disagree.

between man's material and spiritual commitments. As Jesus put it, "For where your treasure is, there will your heart be also." [1]

While the pastors themselves gave high recognition to this underlying connection in human nature, they apparently have not put the point across to the laity.

Another detectable, yet milder difference showed up in the clergy's comparative minimizing of the church's contribution to meeting the "right kind of people." They rated this last on the percentage scale, and also last or next to it for U. S. clergy in the mean scoring. Lay people gave it a higher rating in both instances than their clergy, although putting it next to last both in Canada and the United States. In the declarative terms of the test statement, the laity tended simply to agree that the church has, in fact, helped them "to meet the right kinds of people." But again, they demonstrate that they do not regard this incidental social asset as the primarily important function of the church in their lives.

Canadian lay people were less inclined to ratify the social aspect or any other benefit than were U. S. lay people. Aside from this general distinction, however, the only specifically differentiating factor between them showed up in the relatively higher regard the Canadian lay people give to the church as a "refuge" from life's problems. This suggests they see the church as a more privately oriented institution, focused on individual nurture apart from the wider ambiguities of living. In contrast, it is in the broader context that the clergy of both countries and the U. S. laity see the church.

Classification by age brings out its bearings on the view of needs met through church life.

[1] Matthew 6:21

Among both clergy and laity, the passage of years deepens the appreciation for the benefits of church involvement. The least appreciation is indicated by those under 30, while those over 50 have the keenest sense of these values, as shown in Table 9, page 56.

Scored in the middle zone are clergy and laity between 30 and 49 years of age, who appear as a kind of buffer between the more dubious mood of youth and the firm certainties of age. This intermediate age bracket, ordinarily representing the most determinative and productive years of life, seems to offer a bridge between the questioning early years and the more definite realizations of age.

People of the middle period display sympathies for both ends of the spectrum, doubtlessly often because of their still intimate relationships with youthful offspring, coupled with a growing stability of age. Through this combination of tolerance for innovation and the experienced lessons of years, this group reflects a highly congruous estimate of the church's benefits, and would seem to be the main force for reconciling divergencies within it.

This group's aptitude for identifying with varying shades of interest also makes them pivotal in dealing with pressures for change and in the continuous tasks of readjustments necessary in the church for carrying out its mission most effectively in an ever-fluctuating environment.

BELIEFS IN ACTION

Results of the third set of test statements on faith, designed to bring out the ways in which people put it into practice, are shown in percentages in Table 10, page 57, grouping together as "positive" those who strongly agree, agree or

table 9*

EXPECTATION OF THE CHURCH BY AGES

	Clergy					Laity					
	20-29	30-39	40-49	50-64	65+	14-19	20-29	30-39	40-49	50-64	65+
The church is important to me as a place where I get strength and courage for dealing with the trials and problems of life.	1.93	1.82	1.72	1.61	1.39	2.42	2.01	1.85	1.82	1.73	1.65
Church is important as a place to go for comfort and refuge from the trials and problems of life.	3.00	2.66	2.63	2.07	1.88	2.36	2.24	2.02	1.93	1.89	1.78
Church membership has helped me to meet the right kinds of people.	3.11	2.88	2.87	1.96	1.98	2.87	2.67	2.72	2.51	2.26	1.94
The more I support the church financially, the closer I feel to it and to God.	2.78	2.39	2.23	1.96	1.71	3.86	3.34	3.14	2.81	2.51	2.17

* The lower the score, the stronger agreement, based on a scale of 1 to 6. 1 = strongly agree; 2 = agree; 3 = tend to agree; 4 = tend to disagree; 5 = disagree; 6 = strongly disagree. U.S. only.

table 10*

PRACTICE OF FAITH

	U.S. Clergy positive	U.S. Clergy negative	United Church of Canada Clergy positive	United Church of Canada Clergy negative	U.S. Laity positive	U.S. Laity negative	United Church of Canada Laity positive	United Church of Canada Laity negative
I try hard to grow in understanding of what it means to live as a child of God.	99.6	.4	100	0	97.7	2.3	86.8	13.2
I try hard to carry my religion over into all my other dealings in life.	99	1	96	4	95	5	88.8	11.2
I frequently try to find out what God wants me to do before making decisions in my everyday life.	95.6	6.4	92.9	7.3	89.1	10.9	65	35

* figures in percentages

57

tend to agree, and as "negative" those tending to disagree, disagreeing or strongly disagreeing.

As measured by these statements, the predominant, active ramifications of faith are seeking to "grow in understanding" of fidelity to God and working to apply religious ideals in realms of life beyond the church. General consistency of agreement was registered on these objectives both by clergy and laity, although U. S. clergy display a slightly wider adherence to these aims. The difference, however, remains minimal.

Once again, Canadian lay people show their characteristic trace of individuality, being considerably less sanguine about the effects of faith than others, including their pastors. This could imply less concentration on it, or more likely, a more critically realistic view of actual life situations and human inadequacies in implementing the faith. Also, unlike others, Canadian lay people switch the order of preference, giving precedence to extension of religious values in everyday affairs, with efforts to grow in understanding secondary. The difference here, however, is only by a narrow, perhaps inconsequential margin.

Neither the clergy nor laity in either country indicated as much attention to the third-placed test statement—trying regularly to "find out what God wants me to do" in making everyday decisions. This statement was intended to gauge the reliance on personal devotions or regular prayer for guidance. Although the combined "agreeing" responses show a strong majority espouse this practice, so many only "tended to agree" with it that the more precise mean scores were narrowly within the affirmative range for clergy and U. S. laity, and slightly on the "disagreeing" side for the Canadian laity.

These mean scores on applying the faith, including the comparatively weak affirmations of private devotions about life's decisions, are shown in Table 11. These scores also underline the somewhat more optimistic assertions of U. S. clergy in regard to implementing the faith than shown by their Canadian counterparts. While these mean scores are somewhat harder to visualize, they are more accurate in measuring intensity of attitude. The scores range from one to six, and remember, the lower the score, the keener the agreement.

table 11*

PRACTICE OF FAITH (MEAN SCORES)

	Clergy		Laity	
	U.S.	U.C.C.	U.S.	U.C.C.
I try hard to grow in understanding of what it means to live as a child of God.	1.56	1.82	1.84	2.46
I try hard to carry my religion over into all my other dealings in life.	1.58	1.85	1.88	2.30
I frequently try to find out what God wants me to do before making decisions in my everyday life.	2.00	2.32	2.28	3.08

* Scores up to 3.5 are in the "agree" range.

Once more, the classification of responses by age brought out that in most cases, the practicing implications of faith are more keenly sensed with the passage of years. This is shown, by mean scores, in Table 12 on page 61. One exception appears in the case of clergy under 30 years

59

of age, who most strongly affirm the effort to "grow in understanding" the means of serving God. In the earlier inquiry into general faith concepts, these younger clergymen also had most strongly affirmed the concept of Christ as a "living reality." Together these parallel reactions indicate a particularly searching, active sensitivity to faith among the younger clergy, boding well for the vitality of the church's future.

In summary, American church people more sweepingly and fully avow the basic beliefs of Christianity than they either find their expectations realized in the church or strive to put that faith into practice. They broadly attest the importance of all three dimensions, but at the same time, the altered degree of affirmation discloses the cutting line between abstract convictions and both human dependence on it and the implementation of it. Declared dedication to theological beliefs comes readily and almost all-inclusively, but when it comes to specifying the resources drawn from it and the active application of it amid the distraction and pressures of living, a note of hesitancy appears. It is not stark or dramatic, but it is there, subtly felt, particularly by the laity.

Another element, recurring throughout the examination of faith and its implications, is the special image that comes through of Canadian laity, members of the trans-Protestant United Church of Canada. In each aspect of the study, their distinctive outlook emerged, varying from that of the U. S. laity and usually from that of their own clergy. They're generally less inclusively definitive about their avowals, more reserved, less assertively positive, perhaps more inwardly self-critical or conscious of the fragility of verbal affirmations.

Part of the difference probably stems from the

table 12*

PRACTICE OF FAITH BY AGE

	Clergy				Laity				
	20-29	30-39	40-49	50-64	65+	14-19	20-29	30-39	40-49	50-64	65+
I try hard to grow in understanding of what it means to live as a child of God.	1.41	1.56	1.59	1.53	1.59	2.09	1.89	1.89	1.87	1.77	1.75
I try hard to carry my religion over into all my other dealings in life.	1.74	1.64	1.56	1.58	1.44	2.58	2.11	1.99	1.94	1.91	1.80
I frequently try to find out what God wants me to do before making decisions in my everyday life.	2.26	2.20	2.04	1.84	1.73	2.68	2.45	2.39	2.31	2.16	2.03

* Based on a scale of 1 to 6. 1 = strongly agree; 2 = agree; 3 = tend to agree; 4 = tend to disagree; 5 = disagree; 6 = strongly disagree. U.S. only.

differing styles of churchmanship in the two countries, that in Canada grown out of a more settled, formal European background, without the revivalist, sometimes disorderly antecedents to be found in the past of most U. S. denominations. In any case, the outlooks of church people in the two countries differ in various intriguingly delicate ways, the Canadians tending to regard the church more as a "refuge" for private nurture, while U. S. lay people see it chiefly as a center of reinforcement for dealing with problems beyond it.

The data also reveal mutual tendencies within age groups all along the line. Although there are some surprising exceptions, the commitment to beliefs, the awareness of personal sustenance derived from church life and a sense of translating faith into practice increases with maturing years. As might be expected, the younger groups exhibit more uncertainty about most points, although in some significant instances, the younger clergy display the strongest commitments, especially in regard to the living presence of Christ in our day.

Generally, the middle-years group, between 30 and 49, emerge as a tempering influence between the poles of age and seem to offer the key medium for keeping channels open between them as well as for moderating new developments in the church for meeting the responsibilities of continuously new conditions.

Because of the widespread, firm regard expressed for traditional church values and methods, it becomes apparent that advocates of rapid or radical change are apt to encounter considerable frustration and resistance. Indeed, it becomes evident that major change in the church can come smoothly only at a moderate, deliberate pace, in view of the high attachment to cherished, familiar custom. In any case, the midway age group stands as the chief potential conciliator of that process.

Overall, however, American Protestants strongly uphold their faith in its classic fundamentals, and while sensing their own shortcomings, find themselves fortified for life through the church and seek to project their faith into everyday affairs. Clergymen are more consistently sure of this total working framework of faith than laity, perhaps because their vocation itself makes them less subject to the counterforces felt by lay people. This, perhaps, may account in part for the laity's more frequent reservations. If this is a possible ground for tension, however, it also is an area for greater guidance, teaching and mutual edification.

PSYCHOLOGICAL ORIENTATIONS

Emphatically, church people bespeak good cheer. They say they're happy, enjoy their work, have found satisfying goals and clear aims in life. These were among the overriding findings of a psychological phase of the study testing the general disposition and mood of Christians. The old canard about church folks wearing long faces and being obsessed with the tragic aspects of existence just doesn't wash, as far as they see it. Rather, they're full of beans and aglow about life and its possibilities.

In a cultural climate in which psychologists say that "existential ennui"—a sense of meaningless apathy—is one of the most widespread emotional problems encountered nowadays, the pervasive mood of lively purpose among church people suggests a wellspring of powerful spiritual vigor working in that group. The avowed feeling of significance and satisfaction in everyday work also seems to counter impressions that people have become depersonalized, no longer seeing any point in their own efforts. In any event, most church members don't see their lives in those bleak terms.

Furthermore, they largely reject the negative attitudes of nullity and chaotic meaninglessness in their lives. However frustrating or confusing circumstances may be, church members affirm they're glad to be involved and feel it is with good cause. Their reactions to the test statements are shown by percentages in Table 13, page 65, with those strongly agreeing, agreeing or tending to agree grouped under "positive" and those strongly disagreeing, disagreeing or tending to disagree classified under "negative."

Clergy agree more often than laity that they have a clear purpose in life. Those in the United States are more sure of it than those in Canada. Canadian laity, with their characteristic reservations, aren't quite as sure as others. Remarkably, there is near unanimity in all categories about daily work being a source of pleasure and satisfaction. When it comes to the broader idea of life being full of joy and satisfaction, however, church people in the United States are more inclusively certain of it than those in Canada.

In response to the negative statements about life being uncontrollable and meaningless, lay people in both countries confess to more feelings along this line than do clergy. In both cases, however, the vast majority disclaim such attitudes. Only a tiny fraction accept the extreme negative view that they often wish they had never been born. The overwhelming proportion of the people relish their living. They don't feel that they're running amuck, tossed about inescapably hither and yon by blind forces or that life has no real significance. They're convinced

table 13*

PSYCHOLOGICAL ORIENTATIONS

	U.S. Clergy		United Church of Canada Clergy		U.S. Laity		United Church of Canada Laity	
	positive	negative	positive	negative	positive	negative	positive	negative
I have discovered satisfying goals and a clear purpose in life.	97.9	2.1	99	1	94.2	5.8	87.5	12.5
Facing my daily tasks is usually a source of pleasure and satisfaction to me.	96	4	94.9	5.1	93.7	6.3	92.2	7.8
My life is full of joy and satisfaction.	94.9	5.1	93	7	93.2	6.8	84.5	15.5
Most of the time my life seems to be out of control.	12.2	87.8	91.8	8.2	23.6	76.4	20.9	79.1
My personal existence often seems meaningless and without purpose.	7.3	92.7	2	98	22	78	23.4	76.6
I often wish I had never been born.	1.9	98.1	2	98	5.9	94.1	7.1	92.9

* figures in percentages

of its inherent meaning and find satisfaction in it.

Nevertheless, the small minority makes plain that the painful questions are present, though seldom overtly.

In the breakdown by ages, the data indicate that older persons both among clergy and laity are more aware of purpose and goals and find more satisfaction in their lives than younger people. These figures, shown in Table 14, page 67, are recorded in mean scores. The lower the score, the stronger is the agreement with the test statements, and the higher the score, the stronger the disagreement, on a scale from one to six.

On the negative statements about life seeming out of control, meaningless and so dismal that it would seem better not to have been born, the two ends of the age scale—the quite young and the quite old—are most inclined to have these hopeless feelings. The same accentuated ache of youth and old age also exists for the clergy. The people of middle years rarely report suffering from it.

The most consistently positive responses are from those between 30 and 49 years. Persons in their thirties appear to be more sure of themselves and more confident about life than any other age group. Obviously, conditions involved in the life cycle itself, from youth through old age, have something to do with people's psychological orientation toward it. There are the common traumatic strains of the teen-agers and those in their early twenties, when decisions usually are made about occupation and a marriage partner. Different anxieties are felt by those in their fifties as they reach their occupational apexes and their children leave home for good. However, the pressures seem to subside for those beyond retirement age as their occupa-

table 14*

PSYCHOLOGICAL ORIENTATIONS BY AGE

	Clergy					Laity					
	20-29	30-39	40-49	50-64	65+	14-19	20-29	30-39	40-49	50-64	65+
I have discovered satisfying goals and a clear purpose in life.	1.93	1.80	1.66	1.54	1.44	2.52	2.15	2.06	1.96	1.95	1.86
Facing my daily tasks is usually a source of pleasure and satisfaction to me.	1.90	2.01	2.01	1.79	1.66	2.59	2.22	2.10	2.05	1.97	1.87
My life is full of joy and satisfaction.	2.00	2.01	2.05	2.03	1.88	2.49	2.18	2.09	2.18	2.19	2.05
Most of the time my life seems to be out of control.	4.67	4.82	4.71	4.65	4.61	4.00	4.33	4.52	4.35	4.23	4.17
My personal existence often seems meaningless and without purpose.	5.07	5.05	5.13	4.98	4.98	4.21	4.65	4.80	4.55	4.29	4.16
I often wish I had never been born.	5.41	5.49	5.59	5.58	5.44	4.88	5.42	5.49	5.48	5.24	4.83

* Scored from one to six, with 1 =strongly agree; 2 = agree; 3 = tend to agree; 4 = tend to disagree; 5 = disagree and 6 = strongly disagree. U.S. only.

tional concerns fade and they adjust to the inevitability of death.

While persons in their thirties and forties experience the usual round of problems and crises, the critical phase apparently comes before and after that middle period. Here again, the middle group reflects a stability and balance between the nostalgia of age and the restive discontent of the young. Those middle years appear to be a time when reality seems closest to the dream.

At the same time, lay people in this category are most preoccupied with activities beyond the church. Those with more time to give the church, the younger and older people, tend most to lack a positive view of satisfying purpose. Yet they also seem most to need the church's help. This situation points to a heavy responsibility on the clergy of middle years for balancing the program in the church to strengthen those who particularly need it.

TESTS OF TOLERANCE

Another set of test statements in the psychological phase of the inquiry sought to bring out the degree of tolerance or lack of it by which people confront ambiguity in life. The results, as shown in Table 15, page 69, indicate that clergymen are markedly more tolerant of diffuse factors in life than lay people. Canadian clergy display the broadest acceptance of diversity, while both Canadian clergy and laity express considerably more acceptance of it than their counterparts in the United States.

What leaps out from these data is the conspicuous difference between clergy and laity in both countries. Quite clearly, lay people are more prone to arbitrary standards and judgmental views than clergy. While a majority of lay peo-

table 15*

TOLERANCE OF AMBIGUITY

	U.S. Clergy		United Church of Canada Clergy		U.S. Laity		United Church of Canada Laity	
	positive	negative	positive	negative	positive	negative	positive	negative
A person either knows the answer to a question or he doesn't.	30.4	69.6	10.2	89.8	50.1	49.9	44.2	55.8
One can classify almost all people as either honest or crooked.	19.9	80.9	9.2	90.8	32.5	67.5	22.2	77.8
There is only one right way to do anything.	17.7	81.3	8.2	91.8	41.1	58.9	35.5	64.5
There are two kinds of people in the world: the weak and the strong.	17.9	82.1	8.1	91.9	42.6	57.4	38.8	61.2

* figures in percentages, with strongly agree, agree and tend to agree grouped as positive and strongly disagree, disagree and tend to disagree grouped as negative.

ple in nearly all instances allow for the indeterminate element in human nature and its ways, a strong minority rejects it. They tend to see life in sheer "blacks" and "whites" rather than in the "greys" that commonly characterize it.

More than 40 percent of the laity in the United States and more than 35 percent in Canada feel there is "only one right way to do anything," that a "person either knows the answer to a question or he doesn't" and that humanity is made up of only two kinds of people, "the weak and the strong." In one case, a bare majority of U. S. laity approved the statement implying only one "answer" to every question. This item also drew sizable concurrence, but less than a majority, from other groups, clergy and laity. In every other instance, majorities of each group, including the U. S. laity, refused to take a rigidly categorical view of human beings or their opinions. They left room for the contingent quality in man and his understandings.

Among lay people, they most strongly rejected the notion that nearly everyone can be classified as "either honest or crooked," doubtlessly reflecting the laity's experience in a secular atmosphere of ambiguous ethics, where, as Reinhold Niebuhr once put it, the best choice is rarely completely right but only of the lesser evil. Clergy also heavily rejected, even more so than laity, the idea that most people are definitively "honest or crooked." However, the clergy gave its most thorough-going rejection to the pigeonholing of people into two types, "weak and strong." The ambiguity of those terms in reality is a recurring point in Scripture, which notes that even "God chose what is weak in the world to shame the strong." [2] And Jesus, the submissive victim,

[2] 1 Corinthians 1:27

turned out to be not so weak. As he put it, "Judge not, that you be not judged." [3]

The graphic point that emerges in this phase of the study is the considerable dichotomy between clergy and laity. While the popular, superficial picture of the clergy, frequently conveyed by fiction and film, is of a pious, chastizing voice of judgment, it turns out that clergymen are much less judgmental than lay people, more open to unseen values in divergent answers, in flawed actions and failing people, despite the ostracizing labels, and much readier to accept the paradoxes, complexities and contradictions that so often mask the truth in human life. The censorious, finger-pointing "preacher," so commonly satirized in American lore, turns out to be another flagrant misrepresentation. Instead, the ordinary, workaday lay people, the barber, businessman and mechanic, those who have sometimes tended to isolate the clergy into a separate, exactingly "righteous sphere" removed from the clouding perplexities of life, actually turn out to be more arbitrarily demanding than the man in the pulpit.

Once again, this raises questions about the effectiveness of communications between clergy and lay people, pointing to a noticeable difference in attitude between them. It also indicates how tensions may arise and how the clergy, as intermediaries, may blur the understanding by denominational personnel of local situations and tempers.

The breakdown by ages on the tolerance tests, Table 16 on page 73, indicates that as people age, they tend to become more "set" in their judgments and less tolerant of divergency or ambiguity. However, in the various age brackets,

[3] Matthew 7:1

the main difference stands out between clergy and laity. In most cases, clergymen between 50 and 64 are more tolerant even than the youngest lay people, who, nevertheless, remain more so than their elders.

CONCLUSIONS

From the tests of core convictions, the benefits people find through church participation, the ways in which they practice their faith and their psychological dispositions toward life and other people, it is clear that American Protestants are more positive about belief itself than any of the other aspects. The living and application of it becomes more problematic. Yet these working consequences also are a highly cherished and genuine ramification of their faith. Older persons take a somewhat sequestered, passive view of church life, but nevertheless, the vast preponderance of members see the church as a kind of power-generating station to equip them to surmount the difficulties of everyday living. They also strongly attest that they work to project their religious principles into the wider realms of life.

A striking point that the study brings out is the comparatively scanty importance attached to devotional life, to regular prayer for guidance. This practice seems to be at an ebb both in the pew and pulpit. It is a time-honored adjunct to worship and to live Christianity, and special efforts to buttress it might help assuage the stresses that sometimes beset congregations. An old Quaker custom of high repute is to approach any differences with prayer for "light." It's hard, in such an atmosphere, to keep squabbling.

In their general outlook on life, church people assert a hearty buoyancy, a certitude about goals

table 16*

TOLERANCE OF AMBIGUITY BY AGE

	Clergy					Laity					
	20-29	30-39	40-49	50-64	65+	14-19	20-29	30-39	40-49	50-64	65+
A person either knows the answer to a question or he doesn't.	4.11	4.28	4.14	3.84	3.68	3.72	3.74	3.67	3.51	3.25	3.04
One can classify almost all people as either honest or crooked.	4.89	4.75	4.74	4.14	4.32	4.65	4.64	4.44	4.12	3.85	3.45
There is only one right way to do anything.	5.22	5.01	4.78	4.46	4.05	4.33	4.46	4.23	3.94	3.45	2.88
There are two kinds of people in the world: the weak and the strong	4.96	4.73	4.73	4.32	3.98	4.10	4.30	4.14	3.88	3.39	2.84

* Scored from 1 to 6, with 1 = strongly agree; 2 = agree; 3 = tend to agree; 4 = tend to disagree; 5 = disagree; 6 = strongly disagree. U.S. only.

and an inner assurance of the worth and meaning of everyday activities. This sense of the basic validity of their lives, in the midst of a widely reported mood of dehumanization and discounted individuality, sounds a vigorous testimony to the psychological health of Christian people. Of course, it can be partly a projection of desires rather than reality, reflecting a human tendency to avoid unpleasantness by denying it. But even allowing for this, the weight of the data indicates a high level of satisfaction and serenity.

While the clergy sanction greater tolerance than the laity, this may be partly an abstract, philosophical kind of tolerance, a mode in which clergymen are accustomed to thinking. Lay people don't display it in nearly as thorough a fashion. Nevertheless, on a concrete point of tolerance brought out in an earlier section of this report, a fourth of the lay people preferred not to specify whether withholding contributions from the church could be justified, choosing to offer a nebulous answer of "it depends." In other words, they were inclined to leave latitude for diversity. This sort of specific tolerance sometimes may be more real than that of theoretical understanding. Throughout the study, instances occurred in which active tolerance was displayed simultaneously with verbal depreciations of it.

Contrasts in national attitudes also are frequent. Canadians, whose institutional image of the church differs somewhat from the more personally proprietary view held in the United States, display a greater detachment and analytical stance toward it than do U.S. lay people. However, Canadian pastors are more definitely sanguine about it, often matching the ardor demonstrated by U. S. laity and pastors.

Yet, all along the way, the data show distinct

gradations between clergy and laity in both countries. This is an age-old problem, one which the Protestant Reformation sought to resolve by erasing the sharp demarcations between clergy and laity. Much effort, discussion and exhortation still go into that cause, asserting the interlinked identity and cohesive teamwork of clergy and laity. Yet the disparities of understanding remain apparent.

This seems a challenge and an opportunity to American Protestantism to make its egalitarian heritage more real, its communal coherence more complete. It calls, on both sides, for candor.

3.

parish expectations

Drops fill the ocean. Blades form the grass. Bricks constitute the houses. And persons make up the church. The church is an intimate entity, an immediately personal, directly associated companionship of specific people in specific places. "Where two or three are gathered in my name," Jesus put it.[1] These particular, spatially delimited units are the raison d'être of the denominations. The larger organization issues from that underlying residential base, from the bottom up, not from the top down. The denomination would have no existence, no reality without its local components. They are the vital cells, the lifeblood and flesh of Christian continuity. They are its soil, its fibers, its growth and its fruits. They give it being.

And they encompass the land, these individualized, commingled companies. They inhabit every town in America. From sea to sea, the cross-tipped spires of their structures notch the skyline. They nestle on neighborhood streetsides, hunch resolutely in the teeming downtowns, peep from the hedged driveways of the suburbs. They are a many-faceted lot. Neat, halcyon sanctuaries and towering, colonnaded tabernacles, roughhewn, one-room meeting houses and majestic cathedrals, tasteful little chapels

[1] Matthew 18:20

and bronze-domed temples with "drive-in" parking spaces, audio-equipped. They span the continent, 300,000 of them in the United States, 20,000 in Canada, dotting the cities, occupying the villages and rural crossroads, from the hills of Tennessee to the metropolitan avenues, the variegated, multiplex body of the church.

It is a tremendous network, but its substance is the local congregation, the "brethren and sisters," the individual bands of believers of myriad kinds and many places. As they fare, so fares the church. Their work is the work of Christianity. Their participation, support and understanding determine the church's viability and its impact in the world.

Just what are they up to? What do these folks want of their local churches and their denominations? Where are the main tasks and aims? What do the participants think their parishes should be doing, the operational objectives? What purposes draw them together and what, in some instances, causes members to drop out and drift away? What assistance do these groups expect from the denominations? How do they feel about nearby congregations of other names and denominational lineage? Do they want cooperation with them? Do they feel tribally separate and special, or joined in common cause with other Christians?

These questions, explored in this study, are at the heart of some of the chronic problems of that strangely immense and remote, yet basically small and familiar organism called the church. Its localized nature is part of its genius and also its liability. By its localism, the church is enabled to convey its ideals, reassurance and comradeship directly to persons where it counts, to deal with their particular needs within their own communities, which they influence and help shape and give direction. But at the same time, the localized characteristic leaves the way open to provincial biases, to blocking off learning from the rest of Christianity, to ensnarement by partisan leaders or narrow causes, to distortions of the Gospel itself under the sway of regional mores or surrounding social pressures. Parochialism is the church's balm, but also can be its bane.

The findings of this study bring out some of the weaknesses, and also the strengths.

A general point that emerged combines both elements—a potentiality for more inclusive personal involvement that seems not fully tapped. Members predominantly indicated their eagerness to share in planning and developing the congregation's activities. Yet in many instances, this responsibility largely has been taken over by a key few, an inner circle of clergy and close associates who run the budget and program, generally on the assumption that the mass of members are apthetic and disinterested. But the data in this study refute that notion, emphasizing that most members are concerned and want a hand in shaping and carrying out the church's undertakings. They may feel unneeded and unwanted, but they care, and would like to act it.

TASKS OF THE LOCAL CHURCH

The diversified ministry of Jesus included teaching, prayer and particular attention to hunger, illness, poverty, the outcasts and the lost. He shunned the affluent, Roman-empowered establishment, concentrating on the lowly and rejected. At the same time, he gradually let his secret become known to a few closest to him, and eventually, after his resurrection, many others came to recognize his will and ways as those of

78

God and that his work offered the means of fulfillment for all humanity.

Now, 2,000 years later, what do his followers think the local churches should be doing to perpetuate that ministry?

They assert, first and foremost, that it is to expand acknowledgment of him and trust in him, to convince ever greater numbers of the sacred identity he bore, to "win others to Christ." A heavy preponderance of lay people and clergymen in the United States cited this as the local church's paramount duty, their numbers overweighing the majority of Canadian pastors and laity who felt that the prime task of the local church is to "provide worship for members." This was rated second by U. S. laity and clergy.

Other functions regarded of high-level but descending importance included supplying religious instruction to members, providing ministerial services, helping the needy and administering the sacraments. These were among the top six tasks chosen from among 14 possibles as shown in Chart 1 on page 80.

However, the picture is not as clear-cut as the blanket gradings might imply. Here, in this vital matter of the central aims of the church, the mark of regionalism and local conditions becomes apparent. In this case, it is not a deep or decisive imprint and on the whole only slight, yet enough to show that geography sometimes shades religion.

The differences seem to arise from varying lifestyles, the manner and situations in which people live. This involves their economic status, whether they can afford to travel, their education, occupation, the amount of leisure time they have and how they use it and also importantly, their locale, its anxieties and habits, its cultural resources, density of population, even its types

79

CHART 1

Most important things a local church does

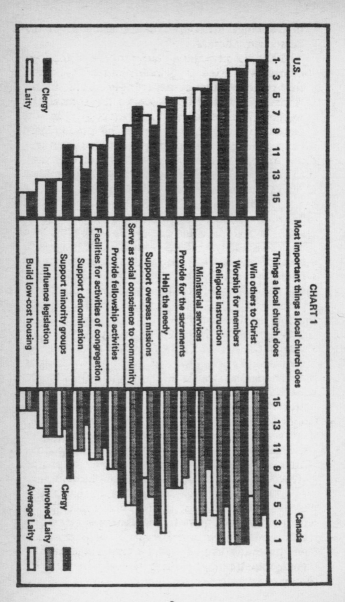

U.S.

Legend: ■ Clergy □ Laity

Scale: 1 · 3 · 5 · 7 · 9 · 11 · 13 · 15

Things a local church does:

- Win others to Christ
- Worship for members
- Religious instruction
- Ministerial services
- Provide for the sacraments
- Help the needy
- Support overseas missions
- Serve as social conscience to community
- Provide fellowship activities
- Facilities for activities of congregation
- Support denomination
- Support minority groups
- Influence legislation
- Build low-cost housing

Canada

Scale: 15 · 13 · 11 · 9 · 7 · 5 · 3 · 1

Legend: ■ Clergy ▓ Involved Laity □ Average Laity

of dwellings, whether urban apartments or dispersed rural homes.

While the prevailing chief purpose of the local church was listed as "winning others to Christ," this priority loomed surpassingly strong in the relatively small churches across the central and western United States and especially in the South. In contrast, it was not the predominant concern of churches of more than 500 members, nor of the churches, large or small, of the country's heavily metropolitan northeastern region. They, like the Canadian clergy and laity, put the main accent on worship rather than evangelism.

The contrasts, by size of church and region, are shown in Tables 17 and 18 on pages 82 and 83. The scores are based on selections from a list of 14 possible local church functions of the six considered most important, in the order of their priority. The results are scaled from 1 to 7, with the lowest scores indicating the highest proportion of top preferences.

Why these differing evaluations? It could be simply the echoes of regional patterns, the expression of tendencies long prevalent within the diverse social milieus. More likely, however, there are conditions inherent in those environments that lead to particular religious leanings.

Notably, the data show that it is the small, often rural churches that most invariably stress the primacy of "winning others." In a strictly practical sense, this could be a way of saying "we need more members" for the church's sake as a matter of self-preservation. Urbanization has drained the rural populations, especially of its young, leaving churches in some sparse areas hard pressed for membership. These churches are generally avoided by better trained clergymen, sometimes go without a full-time minister

table 17*

RESPONSE BY CHURCH SIZE TO THE MOST IMPORTANT THINGS A LOCAL CHURCH DOES.

	no response	less than 150	150- 249	250- 299	300- 499	500- 749	750- 1,499	1,500- over
Win others to Christ	3.11	2.68	2.85	2.90	2.84	3.50	3.77	3.91
Provide worship for members	3.18	3.77	3.67	3.58	3.68	3.48	3.40	3.24
Provide religious instruction	4.31	4.46	4.30	4.35	4.31	4.30	4.41	4.09
Help the needy	5.49	4.87	4.99	5.02	5.19	5.11	4.95	5.28
Provide ministerial service	5.13	5.10	5.06	4.96	4.93	5.01	4.75	4.62
Provide for the sacraments	5.22	5.34	5.07	5.32	4.97	5.23	5.29	5.40
Support overseas missions	6.08	5.77	6.03	5.85	5.93	5.79	5.90	5.83
Provide fellowship activities	6.44	5.94	6.03	6.12	6.09	5.97	6.11	6.03
Serve as social conscience to community	4.90	5.95	5.82	5.87	5.90	5.76	5.44	5.48
Provide facilities	6.38	6.31	6.33	6.44	6.32	6.33	6.23	6.16
Support minority groups	6.42	6.61	6.73	6.69	6.73	6.64	6.63	6.64
Influence legislation	6.84	6.82	6.79	6.74	6.80	6.72	6.77	6.81
Build low-cost housing	6.96	6.91	6.92	6.85	6.90	6.80	6.84	6.94
Support denomination	6.35	6.45	6.43	6.37	6.41	6.48	6.53	6.56

* Responses graded 1 to 7, according to priority given each task. The lower the score, the higher the priority.

table 18*

MOST IMPORTANT THINGS LOCAL CHURCH DOES

	Metropolitan				Non-Metropolitan			
	S	NE	NC	W	S	NE	NC	W
Win others to Christ	2.41	3.38	3.05	2.82	2.10	3.26	2.83	3.03
Provide worship	3.54	3.29	3.54	3.97	3.71	3.52	3.52	3.07
Provide religious instruction	4.23	4.43	4.32	4.24	4.39	4.30	4.17	4.10
Provide ministerial service	4.89	4.72	4.98	4.81	4.95	4.95	4.96	4.77
Help the needy	5.04	5.25	5.23	5.12	4.54	4.85	5.41	5.58
Provide sacraments	5.07	5.00	4.80	5.37	5.16	5.38	5.00	5.16
Social conscience to community	5.96	5.84	5.83	5.88	5.96	5.75	5.98	6.18
Provide fellowship	6.21	5.98	6.26	5.97	6.06	6.09	6.11	5.91
Support overseas missions	6.24	6.01	6.02	5.79	5.91	5.98	5.91	5.84
Support denomination	6.45	6.44	6.48	6.36	6.47	6.26	6.34	6.07
Provide congregational activities	6.46	6.34	6.34	6.37	6.48	6.21	6.39	6.26
Support minority groups	6.75	6.68	6.55	6.67	6.80	6.57	6.76	6.78
Influence legislation	6.83	6.76	6.76	6.85	6.79	6.83	6.80	6.87

* Responses scaled 1 to 7, according to priority given each task. The lower the score, the higher the priority. U.S. only.

and frequently are impelled to consolidate with other congregations to survive. In such circumstances, "winning others" can become doubly urgent, not only for the welfare of others, but for that of the organization.

However, it is not only moderate or minimal church size that heightens concentration on evangelism. This also is an exceptionally strong regional emphasis in the South, known for its widespread revival meetings in churches large and small. Its church people gave a more overwhelmingly first rating to that concern than did any other area. Blacks also, with their extensive roots in the South, rated "winning others" more thoroughly as the main function than did either America's whites or those of Spanish background. Something in the southern ethos, aside from its many smaller country churches, makes seeking newly accepting adherents a preeminent preoccupation, perhaps having to do with its own remembered separation and a resultant passion for acceptance.

Both in metropolitan and non-metropolitan regions of the South, the absorption in "winning others" exceeds that of other regions. The West follows closely in line, displaying a kindred disposition.

On the other hand, a differing consideration appears in the northeastern United States with its older, stabler concentrations of population. Here, the principal function of the local church is regarded as "providing worship" for members, rather than soliciting new ones. The same estimate prevails in Canada, and predominantly in both countries in the larger congregations, those with more than 500 members. As shown in Table 17, the focus by the big churches is on worship rather than expansion.

Here again, we confront that puzzling imprint

of place and situation. What causes it? The highly urbanized areas, with their congestion, their impersonal high-rise apartment dwellings, their isolating patterns of work and living, tend to overshadow individuality. The lonely walk unnoticed in the crowds and the anonymous stranger goes uninvited. It might be that this atmosphere inclines the metropolitan Northeast and the bigger churches to be more concerned with maintenance of congregational worship than with recruiting those beyond the fold, who often may seem a blurred, protean swarm, virtually immune to contact or welcoming word.

In contrast, the South and West have a reputation for greater personal warmth, hospitality and eager hand-clasping friendliness, whatever its psychological origins. Just as those characteristics and their more extensive prevalence in the South and West, as well as in the smaller churches, may add to the push for "winning others," so may subreligious practicalities of the megalopolitan horde seem to modify that concern in the bigger churches and those of the impacted Northeast, focusing interest on worship and the Gospel's implications for living.

Aside from region, other general factors also affected the assessments. Overall, clergy gave weightier importance to "winning others" than laity; older persons of both categories are more dedicated to it than their younger colleagues. Indeed, the youngest clergy—those under 30—minimized "winning others" down in fifth place rather than first, concentrating their choices on worship as foremost, along with teaching and social implementation of the Gospel. Quite differently, blacks regarded worship as definitely subsidiary, putting it down in fourth place, giving the highest import to "winning others." Next to that, in second place, blacks cited "helping the needy," displaying a keener sensitivity to their plight than any others, possibly more closely matching the model set by Jesus.

Despite the peripheral differences, however, a consistent keynote, a common chord, stands out in regard to the main objectives of the congregation. In total, for all areas and groups, the cardinal concern is meditating on the message of Jesus, persuading others to believe and trust his unique authority and way. Even in regions and cultural settings that cite instead the priority of worship, they still regard "winning others" as the next most salient obligation. Furthermore, even this difference could be largely one of semantics and usage. In essence, worship and drawing others into it are interwoven parts of one process, both directed toward infusing life with a greater sense of meaning and worth. Both are forms of evangelism, of learning and growing, whether through pulpit proclamation or common prayer. Just as "winning others" implies instilling people with a deeper awareness of the realities of faith, so is worship aimed at inculcating and heightening that experience and attracting others to it.

In that broad sense, American churches north and south, rural and urban, are of a common mind about it—that their prime task is to bring people together in a context that will influence and enrich their lives. This, as they see it, is the supreme responsibility, the central mandate.

Beyond this, the next most important function, technically in third place, is providing religious instruction. This is a particularly keen concern of lay people between the ages of 20 and 50, including those of child-rearing ages wanting their young trained in the faith. Members over 65 are not so interested in study as others, but still give it prominent rating. Whites stress classwork more than Spanish Americans, who, in turn, are more interested in it than blacks. Aside from the variations, however, the vast majority see Christian education as a vital adjunct. They regard themselves as a people of the Book and recognize that if they're going to convey it responsibly, they've got to dig into it.

Next and fourth in importance among functions of the local church, Americans (with the exception of Canadian clergy) listed "ministerial services." This normally means pastoral calls, counseling, preaching, leading worship and conducting various religious rites such as marriages and funerals. Big churches, those of more than 750 members, considered these functions more important than smaller congregations, reflecting their more informal leadership and less structured life-style. The metropolitan Northeast also put more emphasis on "ministerial services" than other regions.

Curiously, in a class of their own, Canadian clergymen minimized the professional role, dropping it into eighth place. This relegated it below the seventh place given it by blacks, and above the ninth place accorded it by Spanish Americans. Probably the casual, spontaneous churchmanship among black and brown-skinned Christians accounts for this downplaying of ministerial services. Younger whites in the age groupings showed similar tendencies. But apart from them and the Canadian clergy, whites generally esteem the pastoral helps more highly.

Below fourth place, the rankings of local-church functions become nebulous and mixed, varying by groups and regions. On the average, "helping the needy" and providing the sacraments, chiefly baptism and the Lord's Supper, came fifth and sixth in the ratings. However, the cases of differences from these general norms offer the more fascinating notes.

For instance, the local church's duty to "serve as a social conscience to the community" was ranked fourth by Canadian pastors, sixth by Canadian laity and U. S. pastors, and at least a notch above that by clergy under 50, by black and Spanish American lay people. But it was depreciated to eighth place by U. S. lay people generally. They're more concerned about ministerial services and sacraments, although they also accord about equal importance to "helping the needy." Compared to their clergymen, to blacks and Canadian lay folk and pastors, the U. S. lay people are not so disposed for the local church to act as a collective instrument of social justice —a job they're prone to relay to the denomination. Older members, those over 50, and smaller churches, those under 150 members, are even less inclined than others for the local congregation to take on community social issues. Frailties of age and scanty memberships may deter them from the strains of it.

Nevertheless, considering the thorny, often controversial nature of that function, it showed considerable strength, ranking in the upper-six brackets for most classifications, higher than that for the vigorous but mature clergy under 50, and midway in the overall list even by U. S. laity.

Another interesting sidelight appears in the considerable support that lay people attach to "supporting overseas missions." Both in Canada and the United States, they rate this as the seventh most urgent task, a point higher than the U. S. clergy's lesser estimate of it. But Canadian clergy give it a point more significance even than the laity. Along racial lines, Spanish Americans rate it higher than any group, in sixth place, indicating their concern for brethren in Latin America. In contrast, the youngest clergy both in Canada and the United States, those under 30, relegate overseas missions to eighth place. They, like blacks, put the focus on helping the needy, considering it second only to worship, and are more interested in implementing Christian ethics in the home community.

As in other cases, age, circumstances and racial background often shift the balance one way or another on the scale, but generally, aside from a few marked divergences in smaller segments of congregational life, American Christians display an essentially compatible scale of criteria for their labors. Despite the variations up and down the spectrum, these usually were minor, only rarely sharp, and with the topmost focus on worship and evangelism. This was followed by an upper half dozen other salient concerns, even though sometimes in slightly differing sequence, embracing the main tasks for the local church as seen by virtually all regions, ages, races and economic levels.

There are, of course, intriguing distinctions. Blacks, browns and younger white Christians aren't as zealous about professional ministerial services as most whites. And blacks aren't as dedicated to religious study as whites, displaying a greater propensity for action, for helping the needy, which also is a higher concern of younger clergymen. However, blacks join with most southerners and central and western whites, as well as with smaller churches, in putting the highest premium on "winning others." While this differs in terminology from the "worship" emphasis of the younger white clergy, the bigger churches and the larger metropolitan sections, the basic intent seems parallel. Further, the other uppermost concerns shown in the study, religious instruction, helping the needy, ministerial services, the sacraments and voicing a social conscience, even if placed in differing orders, are underlined in the various categories of church people.

Out of the 14 possible congregational functions, six others were discounted across the board, including such roles as providing "fellowship activities" and "facilities for activities," supporting the denomination, building low-cost housing, influencing legislation and supporting minority groups, all of them rated below ninth place, except in one instance. The Canadian clergy, those inveterate iconoclasts, ranked "fellowship activities" as seventh. Not so, however, for their lay people or for U. S. clergy and laity, who ranked that function in ninth place, soundly squelching the common jibe that they value the local church as a chummy social clubhouse.

WHY PEOPLE LOSE INTEREST

Twenty-seven percent of the lay people in the United States and 35 percent of those in Canada said they had become less active in their churches within the past three years. A smaller proportion, 24 percent of the U. S. laity and 12 percent of the Canadian laity, said they had become more active in the same period. However, the bulk of church members, 48 percent of those in the United States and 52 percent of the Canadians, felt their level of activity had stayed about the same, steady and on an even keel. This unfluctuating group ranged from the highly involved to the mostly inactive.

To an impressive degree, the biggest share of increased activity was among persons under 30 years of age. More than 42 percent of them said that they had stepped up their activity in the church, nearly twice as big a proportion as for the membership in general, revealing a highly promising impulse among younger people and auguring well for the future vitality of the churches.

On the other hand, the percentage of those whose activity recently has tapered off involves about a third of all church members, a drift both sizable and serious. The main reasons for it, as church people see it, are shown in Table 19, page 92. In this inquiry, people were asked to choose six reasons, in order of importance, out of the 16 listed. Because of their large numbers, the U. S. laity's views dominate the rankings. The rankings are based on a scaling system not shown here; only the sequence of heaviest emphasis is shown, from 1 through the least mentioned cause, 16. For Canadian clergy, analysts there used a conditionally weighted ranking. But for comparative purposes the same scale is applied for them in Table 19 as for U. S. clergy.

The study in Canada included one aspect not attempted in the United States—the separate classifications of attitudes of highly "involved members" and casual "average members." The ranking of clergy emphasis on the various items also was weighted by certain factors. These distinctions, while not greatly affecting the order of most frequent upper choices, are shown pictorially in Chart 2 on page 93.

The outstanding feature of these self-searching explanations for fading involvement in the church is that they are highly personal. They center not so much on the church as on individuals. The predominant reasons for curtailed church activity are simply a lack of time or diversion of it. Americans say it is a matter of people finding themselves without any extra moments left to give the church or so immersed in other organizational affairs that no opportunity re-

table 19*

WHY PEOPLE LOSE INTEREST IN THE CHURCH

People sometimes lose interest in the church even though they may have been quite active. Some possible reasons for this are included on cards. Select six, in order of the most frequent occurrence, which you consider the main reasons for people losing interest.

	U.S.		Canadian	
	Laity	Clergy	Laity	Clergy
No time for church	1	2	2	5
More interested in non-church organizations	2	3	1	3
Dislike pastor	3	8	8	7
Lost faith in church	4	6	5	4
Program not appealing	5	4	4	6
Frequent financial appeal	6	12	6	8
Church not important in modern life	7	1	7	1
Dislike church leaders other than pastors	8	10	14	12
Church people are hypocritical	9	9	11	9
Family members no longer involved	10	5	3	2
Age or ill health	11	11	9	11
Preaching	12	14	10	14
Doctrinal differences with leadership	13	13	13	13
Social involvement of church	14	7	15	15
No social involvement by church	15	15	12	10
Church facilities inadequate	16	16	16	16

* The rankings given here, in order of most significant cause, are based on scale averages from 1 to 7, with reasons getting the heaviest concentration of upper choices attaining the lower score and thus the higher rank. The scores are not shown, only the rankings.

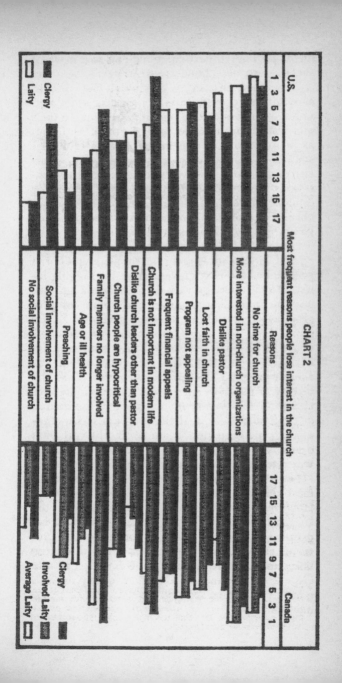

CHART 2

Most frequent reasons people lose interest in the church

Reasons
No time for church
More interested in non-church organizations
Dislike pastor
Lost faith in church
Program not appealing
Frequent financial appeals
Church is not important in modern life
Dislike church leaders other than pastor
Church people are hypocritical
Family members no longer involved
Age or ill health
Preaching
Social involvement of church
No social involvement of church

U.S.
Clergy
Laity

Canada
Clergy
Involved Laity
Average Laity

mains for church participation. This is a mark of the modern age, the "squirrel cage," the press and swirl of distracting demands—job, schools, committees, causes, family projects, schedules, visits, extra work, trips, emergencies, traffic jams and waiting in line. No time, no time. And that, as people see it, is the main pressure tank that squeezes them out of church activity. Both scarcity of time and the rivalry for it of other organizations are listed as the two leading causes for diminished church involvement. Understandably, these two corresponding reasons loom greater for lay people than for pastors.

Other than this competitive drain on time, people cited the lack of an appealing church program as the next gravest cause for sagging interest. The rankings varied for different groups, but the total data underlined drabness of program as slightly ahead of ensuing factors. At the same time, the large proportion of members under 40 who have increased their church activity lately pointed to the attractiveness of the church program as their reason for it. Thus the quality of program emerges as a crucial element, either stirring greater involvement in the church or defections from it. If the program seems stimulating, participation mounts; if the program drags, people edge out. A lackluster program was rated as the third most abrasive deterrent.

Next in line in the overall data as the fourth most alienating factor was dislike for the pastor. However, what elevated its influence was the emphasis on it by the large number of U.S. lay people. They rated it third, above shoddy program. But other groups graded it far down the line, in eighth place for U.S. clergy and Canadian laity and for Canadian clergy, in fifth place by weighted scoring, seventh place for regular scoring.

This sort of differentiation between groups and experiences dominated the ratings below the first three items and offered the most interesting glimpses into particular slants on the matter. For instance, U. S. lay people display a more personally possessive view of the church, tending to assess it in terms of direct interrelationships with others. Considerable importance is attributed to such factors as dislike for the pastor, loss of confidence in the particular church and dislike of its leaders as among factors disenchanting people with it. These interhuman factors are comparatively less influential in Canada, where the drawbacks are seen more in the lure of "non-church activities," the dullness of the program or the fact that "family members are no longer involved."

The differences between the Canadian classifications of "involved" and "average" members show up in their concepts of why some people drop out. The "average" members are more inclined to think that interest declines when "family members are no longer involved." But this spin-off effect of waning family ties isn't considered of such moment by the genuinely "involved" members, who apparently tend to set their own course about the matter rather than being whiplashed by indirect considerations.

In the United States, the problem of "no time for the church" is especially acute for persons under 40, a period when they have a multiplicity of demands on their time including young children, their education and building of careers. For middle-aged adults, those 40 to 64, when commitments have mounted beyond the church, the pull of "non-church activities" takes precedence as an interference with church life. For older retired people, those above 65, "age or ill health" becomes the chief obstacle.

Residential environment also plays a part in these estimates. For non-metropolitan people in the medium-sized and rural towns and people in churches under 500 members, the personal tastes such as dislike for pastor or church leaders are considered more decisive than in the metropolitan areas and in the larger churches of more than 500 members. For them, a seeming nonimportance of the church in modern society and dropping out of family members emerges as more detrimental.

These differences reflect the life-styles of the region—the big-church urban scene in which abstract or incidental influences play a greater part in their wider range of alternative organizations, and the small-church rural scene where the more limited choice of institutions intensifies the insistence on personally suitable relationships within them, including the church, shown in Tables 20 and 21, pages 97 and 98.

Another graphic variation appeared along racial lines. Blacks cited loss of "faith in the church," a feeling that it's not measuring up to its mission, as the main reason for dropouts, contrasting with the main emphasis by whites on lack of time. Whites reduced to fifth place the sense of disappointment in the church's efficacy. Young people and clergy under 30, however, expressed more consciousness of this factor than their elders. Blacks, in keeping with their view that the main problem lies in faltering confidence in the church's performance, followed this up with a related complaint that the next biggest handicap is that "church people are hypocritical." Spanish Americans gave that item the same high billing. But it hardly entered into the consideration of whites, who downgraded it to tenth place. Obviously, blacks have a stronger sense than others of the local church's fallibility as an

table 20*

REASONS PEOPLE LOSE INTEREST IN CHURCH

	Metropolitan				Non-Metropolitan			
	S	NE	NC	W	S	NE	NC	W
No time for church	4.84	4.65	4.81	4.68	5.03	4.61	4.61	4.53
More interested in non-church organizations	4.97	4.88	4.93	4.90	5.04	4.62	4.66	4.90
Program not appealing	5.06	5.51	5.76	5.48	5.34	5.48	5.69	5.26
Dislike pastor	5.18	5.23	5.18	5.44	5.13	5.17	5.07	5.08
Lost faith in church	5.39	5.41	5.30	5.39	5.33	5.56	5.50	5.29
Church not important	5.59	5.41	5.00	5.24	5.63	5.65	5.29	5.38
Dislike church leaders	5.67	5.86	5.85	6.05	5.40	5.62	5.56	5.78
Frequent financial appeals	5.58	6.04	5.59	5.50	5.76	5.78	5.50	5.73
Church people are hypocritical	5.81	5.66	5.79	5.64	5.46	5.76	5.93	5.26
Family no longer involved	5.82	5.48	5.62	5.56	5.94	5.56	5.67	5.71
Preaching	5.89	5.85	5.80	6.09	6.15	5.89	6.05	6.08
Age or ill health	5.95	5.69	6.05	6.14	5.62	5.55	5.75	6.34
Doctrinal differences with church leadership	6.08	5.94	5.92	5.72	6.12	6.22	6.23	5.93
Social involvement of church	6.18	6.18	6.18	6.13	6.14	6.48	6.28	6.27
No social involvement	6.35	6.37	6.30	6.37	6.40	6.49	6.50	6.68
Church facilities inadequate or poor	6.59	6.79	6.77	6.79	6.71	6.67	6.86	6.81

* Scores based on a scale of 1 to 7. The lower the score, the greater the concentration of high rankings. U. S. only.

table 21*

REASONS PEOPLE LOSE INTEREST IN CHURCH

	no response	less than 150	150-249	250-299	300-499	500-749	750-1,499	1,500-over
No time for church	4.80	4.55	4.66	4.75	4.88	4.92	4.78	5.16
More interested in non-church organizations	4.66	4.95	4.92	4.84	4.89	4.58	4.64	4.75
Dislike pastor	5.13	5.17	5.31	5.29	5.10	5.52	5.44	5.43
Lost faith in church	4.82	5.27	5.60	5.44	5.36	5.45	5.29	5.22
Program not appealing	4.00	5.44	5.46	5.44	5.67	5.45	5.25	5.46
Church is not important	3.69	5.52	5.51	5.27	5.44	5.47	5.31	5.28
Church people hypocritical	6.41	5.54	5.80	5.77	5.66	5.89	5.98	5.86
Dislike church leaders	6.56	5.61	5.64	5.75	5.72	5.97	6.14	6.13
Age or ill health	6.51	5.83	5.85	5.89	5.84	5.85	5.88	5.86
Family members no longer involved	5.90	5.84	5.69	5.71	5.55	5.27	5.44	5.29
Frequent financial appeals	5.46	5.94	5.73	5.62	5.59	5.43	5.52	5.62
Preaching	6.31	5.98	5.88	5.94	5.93	6.14	6.03	5.75
Doctrinal differences	6.69	6.10	5.90	6.10	6.08	6.01	6.20	5.99
No social involvement by church	6.44	6.39	6.36	6.27	6.48	6.37	6.09	6.48
Social involvement of church	5.87	6.49	6.29	6.34	6.28	6.37	6.27	5.90
Facilities poor	6.92	6.61	6.66	6.77	6.83	6.78	6.81	6.91

* Scores based on a 1 to 7 scale. The lower the score, the greater the concentration of high rankings.

institution and its weaknesses in dealing with the ills of contemporary life.

However, the most dramatic difference appears in the clergy's conviction that the main hindrance to church participation is a feeling that the "church is not important in modern life." Pastors both in Canada and the United States rated this as the top cause of defections in the regular scorings (although weighted scorings for Canadian pastors narrowly put it into second place). Either way, it was a No. 1 problem in the eyes of the clergy. But lay people in both countries differed sharply, downgrading the idea of the church not being so important to seventh place.

Persons in the West and North Central United States felt that factor more than those in the South and urbanized Northeast. But overall, lay people simply do not see it as a major problem. The clergy consider it the main trouble spot, that an overshadowing cloud is shrinking the importance of the church in modern times. But lay people themselves are scarcely aware of it. So far as they're concerned, the church remains definitely important. It's the subsidiary annoyances that bother them, not the continuing significance of the church itself. They blithely assume that. But not the furrow-browed clergy.

This is a definite "blind spot" in Christianity's professional corps, which assumes that slackened activity among the people stems from reduced regard for the church and its loss of standing in their eyes. Yet actually, that's not the people's gripe at all. They see other difficulties, but scarcely are aware of the sector cited by their pastors. In short, what appears wrong to the clergy is not what's wrong to the laity. Apparently some work needs to be done to get these wires uncrossed.

WHAT THE DENOMINATION SHOULD DO
FOR THE LOCAL CHURCH

As the jointly spawned and nourished creature of the local churches, the denomination is their servant. It is shaped, supplied and directed by them in expectation of service in return. It is the instrument enabling them to act concertedly in many fields, both nationally and abroad, to carry on work cooperatively beyond their individual capability or reach.

In that role, the denomination also is expected to provide aid directly to the local churches, materials and resources that could not be adequately developed alone. Sometimes denominational personnel are not altogether sure just what tasks congregations want done or what sort of help they need. To pinpoint their wishes more exactly, the question was included in this study. Just what do they expect from the umbrella agencies of the denomination?

First and foremost, they depend on the denominations to "provide and train ministers." Both U. S. clergy and laity in both countries agree that this is the prime denominational responsibility to the local church. The task was rated a close second by Canadian clergy. In fact, throughout this phase of the study, clergy and laity generally tended to be in greater accord in their answers than on most other matters. Denominational officers may have their moments of uncertainty, but the home folks are quite clear about it. Their preferences are shown in Chart 3.

Next to running seminaries and keeping the supply of ministers flowing, the denominations are expected to coordinate and channel funds for "mission support" at home and abroad, a duty Canadian pastors put first. Following close together came the tasks of providing "counsel for

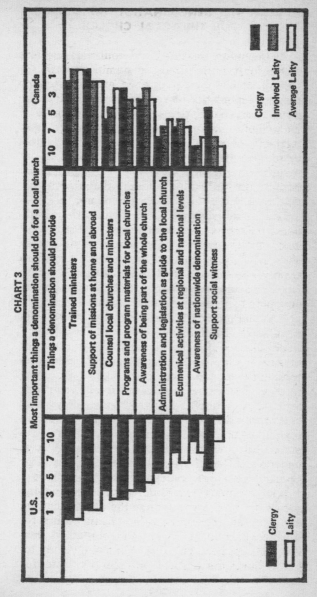

CHART 3

Most important things a denomination should do for a local church

Things a denomination should provide

- Trained ministers
- Support of missions at home and abroad
- Counsel local churches and ministers
- Programs and program materials for local churches
- Awareness of being part of the whole church
- Administration and legislation as guide to the local church
- Ecumenical activities at regional and national levels
- Awareness of nationwide denomination
- Support social witness

U.S. (scale: 1 3 5 7 10)
- Clergy
- Laity

Canada (scale: 10 7 5 3 1)
- Clergy
- Involved Laity
- Average Laity

101

local churches and ministers" and developing "program and resources, including curricula, for local churches."

Incidentally, U. S. laity showed a greater interest in receiving denominational counsel for their local churches than did Canadian laity or clergy of either country. This might seem something of a switch in the usual pattern of the U.S. laity who emphasize a rather proprietary view of their churches. Nevertheless, they're most interested in getting regular advice from their denominational leaders on how to handle their operations, an intimation perhaps that they're not getting as much of it as they would like.

Laity and clergy of both countries indicate high concern with denominational efforts to develop an "awareness of being part of the whole church," of participation in the total Christian enterprise, the universal church-at-large. Probably the somewhat lesser concern shown for denominations engaging in "ecumenical activities at regional and national levels" was simply because of the emphasis on the related, more inclusively phrased dimension. Whatever the connection or overlap here, local congregations clearly want the denominations to illuminate and show forth their involvement in the total breadth of the church's reality.

Interestingly, lay people here assert more concern for ecumenical action than their pastors in both countries. In keeping with this concern, laity as well as the clergy show little taste for promotional efforts to develop an "awareness of nationwide denomination." Obviously, "denomi-nationalism" is not the big thing to them. They're much more concerned with a consciousness of the "whole church" than with puffing up the denominational brand name.

The lowest ranked task of the denomination in

the eyes of the laity is engaging in "social witness" on problems facing society. Clergymen in both countries show a comparatively greater regard for this denominational role than do lay people. However, the discrepancy does not mean that the lay people are against it. In another phase of the study when they were asked specifically whether denominations should speak out on current social issues such as civil rights, war and other problems, 71 percent of them, along with 88 percent of the clergy, responded affirmatively. The difference in this section of the study is that the focus here was on denominational functions performed for the local churches, and from that perspective, the denomination's "social witness" is not among the major local prerequisites. People over 50 felt this more strongly than younger persons.

In the special Canadian breakdown of lay people, the "involved members" showed greater concern than "average members" for development of program materials and training curricula, for ecumenical endeavors and for building up an awareness of being part of the "whole church," thus indicating their keener sense of present institutional processes, particularly in Christian education. Conversely, the "average" members' extra concern for denominational "administration and legislation to guide local churches" and for promoting national denominationalism suggests that they are scantily aware of what the denomination is doing or aren't in tune with it.

Church size also affected responses, with the larger churches, those of more than 300 members, less interested in the denomination providing counsel for them than were the smaller churches. Along with the smaller churches, those in non-metropolitan areas also showed greater appetite for this kind of service. Despite the variations, however, church people generally indicated a lively demand for it.

Oddly, metropolitan area churches felt the need for program and resource material more keenly than churches in more sparsely settled areas. The more rural churches, in turn, give stronger emphasis to the denomination's task of coordinating "mission support" than do their metropolitan brethren. This is a particularly traditional function of denominations and it is ranked first by Spanish Americans, but fourth by blacks, again showing their uneasiness with some traditional ways in the church.

The main distinction between clergy and laity came on the idea of denominational "counsel" to local congregations. Pastors weren't nearly as keen on this as lay people, perhaps because the pastors are more closely in touch with what the denomination is doing and either consider it enough or don't care especially for it. Whatever the reason, the lay people who are least likely to be involved in counsel rendered by denominations are more desirous of it than their pastors.

Among the clergy, Canadians are somewhat less interested than their U. S. counterparts in the denominational role of training ministers and providing administrative guidelines. This seems to reverse the usual image of the U.S. pastors as free-wheeling individualists compared to the Canadian churchmen. For in this case the U. S. clergy display the most concern for ministerial preparation and oversight. Canadian clergy are more interested in ecumenical activities and "social witness" than U.S. parsons.

LOOKING ACROSS THE FENCES

The rise of trans-denominational Christianity is a phenomenon of the present era. It has drastically changed the tone of church diplomacy from one of conflict and competition to increasing operational alliances. And the word runs widely—those who worship one Lord are essentially one. To that end He prayed that "they may all be one . . . so that the world may believe." [2] That long ignored, yet potent idea has become a virtual aphorism of the age, so common it becomes unprovocative. Yet it is profoundly alive and abroad, taking its effects in spreading ways. At the same time, the old denominational walls still stand, thick and entrenched. The separate institutional powers still hold the reins over their domains. Nevertheless,

table 22*

CHURCHES SHOULD WORK TOGETHER

	all respondents	U.S. Clergy	U.S. Laity
strongly agree	49	59.4	46.5
agree	38.9	30.7	40.1
tend to agree	9.5	7.6	10.5
tend to disagree	1.8	1.8	1.8
disagree	.6	.3	.6
strongly disagree	.2	.2	.3

* figures in percentages

[2] John 17:21

at bottom and in the long run, it is the posture of the local people that will mold the future of the denominations. Thus the question arises as to just how they view combined interchurch efforts. The question was put to them—do they think different denominations ought to work together?

Decisively, 97.4 percent of them responded favorably, either strongly agreeing, agreeing or tending to agree. Only a tiny 2.6 percent said no. The pattern held true both for U. S. clergy and laity as shown in Table 22 on page 105.

Translated into local terms, this suggests that denominational identity simply is not a determinative concern of church people today. They still require services and assistance from denominations in doing the work but that basically is simply because denominational structures still mark the lines of Christian organization. "They're all we've got and we have to have them until something better comes along," said a Texas Methodist. In any event, church people overwhelmingly favor the denominations working together. The laity under 50 years of age is more keenly dedicated to this approach than older persons.

In a related question, church members were asked whether they had heard of the National Council of the Churches of Christ in the U.S.A., an interdenominational cooperative organization of 33 Protestant and Eastern Orthodox denominations, and whether the people favored its work. Responses are shown in Table 23, page 107.

The surprise here was that more clergymen— 19.8 percent of them—have unfavorable impressions of the National Council than lay people, only 14.7 percent of them. However, about a fourth of the laity declined to make either a positive or negative judgment since most of them in this group say they know nothing about the ecumenical organization. The negative reac-

table 23*

HAVE YOU HEARD OR READ ABOUT
THE NATIONAL COUNCIL OF CHURCHES?

Much is being said about denominations and churches working together. One way for doing this is through the National Council of Churches. Have you ever heard or read anything about the National Council?

	yes	no	no response
U.S. Clergy	99.3	.4	.4
U.S. Laity	83.6	16	.4

In general, do you have a favorable or unfavorable impression of what they are trying to do?

	favorable	unfavorable	don't know/no response
U.S. Clergy	72.1	19.8	8.1
U.S. Laity	61	14.7	24.3

* figures in percentages

tion goes up slightly with age, to 15.9 percent for those over 50. Among blacks, only a tiny one percent of them are unfavorably disposed toward the Council, a fact doubtlessly mirroring the consistently firm stand that the National Council has taken through the years in support of racial equality.

The overall figures, however, bring out a strange condition surrounding the Council. Ever since it was formed 22 years ago, the word has been widely bruited about, especially in anti-ecumenical circles, that lay people generally were highly irritated at the interdenominational work carried on through it. Opponents have sharply attacked it on the air and in their publications, calling it too inclusive, too liberal, too activist, too concerned with contemporary social ills. Denominational leaders, who make up its policy-making General Board, have squirmed under these barrages, assuming that the people may really feel that the Council is anathema.

However, checking with them shows they don't feel that way to any substantial extent at all. Although a fifth of them have never heard of the organization, an overwhelming majority of those who have look favorably on the Council and most of the others say they don't know enough about it to judge. It's the clergy who are most prone to be critical, just as in some other cases, they show less support for ecumenical activity than do lay people. This is another of those situations in which church leaders, its pastors and its people are entitled to know the truth of the contemporary Christian mood rather than being subjected to distortions of it.

SUMMARY

Summing up, America's churches are chiefly dedicated to that old-time endeavor that never gets old, spreading the Gospel. Sometimes they think of it as pulpit persuasion, of a winning word, a timely nudge. Others see it in the power and pull of the worshiping flock, a community loving the Lord through which meaning is given to lives and the way pointed. Whether they see it in terms of prayer or evangelism, however, it is considered the local church's central imperative by Christians across the continent, black and white, city folks and back countrymen.

Along with that top calling, whites link the pursuit of a firmer grasp of theology, the extension of Christian education to people through instruction. Parents especially emphasize it. But on this point, blacks take a distinctive tack of their own, declaring that helping the needy holds priority over cultivation of the intellect.

Blacks also are more interested than whites in the local church serving as a beacon for social justice in the community. Standing with them on this front are Canadian pastors and laity and to a lesser degree, U. S. clergymen. But U. S. lay people are not inclined to see "social witness" as a responsibility of the local church, considering it instead as a denominational prerogative. In the home church, the U.S. laity expects professional ministerial services, a traditional note that does not appeal so strongly to blacks or young whites. However, the study brings out definitively that Americans don't want their congregations to deteriorate into mere socializing centers, but rather to act as the church under the sway and goal of God.

Nevertheless, they confess to pitfalls within their ranks, to various distractions that can weaken involvement in the church. And the chief problem is seen as that stalking old companion of temporal existence, the inexorable rush of time. It tugs and tosses people about, they say, pressing them this way and that and sometimes hurling them out of church activity. Lesser vexations, such as boring church programs or not getting along with the pastor, also can disenchant members with their churches. These personal distastes are particularly stressed by U.S. laity, although they, along with others, say that the main struggle is with that inescapable crunch of time.

The main vulnerability is not the church itself, however, or its declining significance in modern life as American lay people see it. In this, they firmly disagree with the clergymen, who blame a shrinkage of the church's standing in contemporary culture as the main cause of defections. But this turns out to be a scapegoat so far as lay people are concerned. Despite the clergy's solemn dirges over the church's decline, the lay folk are not highly worried about that. To them, the church still stands solidly. What sets them adrift is mainly the whirligig quality of secular life itself, and not any devaluation of the church.

From the vantage point of the local churches, members see the denomination's main task as training and supplying ministers, along with coordinating mission support on fields beyond the congregation's purview and supplying program and training curricula. While they rely on the denomination for these and other services, most American church members feel that the day of denominational sectarianism is gone and they want their churches to work with others. As a Kentucky Disciples of Christ pastor put it, "If we believe in Christ, we belong to him first rather than to a denomination. We should all stand together as his church."

4.

keys to giving

Americans in 1971 contributed $8.6 billion to religious causes.[1] In the same year, they spent about $30 billion for new cars. Nevertheless, the people's annual investment in church work makes it one of the continent's economically mightiest enterprises next to the government itself, which uses enforced taxation to meet its colossal budget. In contrast, the churches depend entirely on voluntary, free offerings, given without any tangible return, to pay the bills for a worldwide network of mercy and enlightenment —the thousands of church-supported hospitals, schools, orphanages, village development projects, disaster relief operations, theological education centers and missions of training, teaching and technical aid around the globe.

However, local churches spend 80 percent of the total religious revenues on themselves, their own parish upkeep, salaries and activities. About 20 percent is passed on to others to sustain regional, national and international programs.[2]

[1] *Giving, USA, 1972,* the American Association of Fund-Raising Counsel, New York.

[2] *The Yearbook of American Churches, 1972,* based on financial reports from 45 denominations which in 1971 received total donations of $3.8 billion, 80 percent of which was used by local congregations and 20 percent of which went into world benevolences. This fairly steady proportion has edged up slowly in modern times, about two percent in the last decade.

Even this minority share amounts to $1.7 billion, close to recent U.S. foreign aid expenditures. If it should drop by as little as one percent, it would mean a decline of $17 million, forcing curtailment of hundreds of programs, shrinking work at home and abroad, draining capital reserves, forcing withdrawals from the mission field, reducing technical aid projects, cutting back on such worthy operations as medical teams and educational services.

It happened. So did the repercussions.

The crunch hit widely about 1969 and hard. It continued to varying degrees into 1972, with some late signs it was easing up. But over that period, income of some denominations fell more than 10 percent. For others, the squeeze was not so acute, but throughout the religious domain, the financial shock waves forced denominational cutbacks. Church treasurers puzzled over it. Administrators reshuffled structures, pared staffs, lopped off projects and plans and sat through worried conferences trying to figure out what had gone wrong. Various symptoms were cited and theories voiced—the effects of inflation, resistance to the churches' social stance, dismay over doctrinal upheavals, the anti-institutional attitude of the times, a tendency toward insular withdrawal into immediately local concerns and a festering aversion to wider responsibilities in the nation and the world.

The main thesis seemed to be that church people, to a jolting extent, had turned their interests away from the broader church labors to concentrate their resources more heavily on their home parishes. "Expenditures for local operations are at a level never before equaled in the history of the church," the Reverend Dr. Howard Ham, a general secretary of the United Methodist Board of Education, told its 1972 annual meeting. "In contrast, support is being withdrawn from the general funding of operations which the people do not identify as their own special concerns." [3]

Similar views were expressed by many others. The Reverend Dr. Howard E. Spragg, executive vice-president of the United Church of Christ Board of Homeland Ministries, said church members seemed to be pulling back into "religious isolation," abandoning interest in the church's wider mission. "As the church becomes more and more self-centered, it loses its dynamism and reason for existence." He added that while the local congregation is the foundational unit of the church, "insulated localism is a perversion of our faith." [4]

Definite intimations of this home-grounded temperament showed up in the North American church study, yet in noticeably modified ways. The financial strain apparently has been mutual, top and bottom. Moreover, despite some denominational exceptions, nationally inclusive statistics indicate local churches have continued to devote as large a share as before of their revenues to wider denominational endeavors. Actually, the average 20 percent relayed to general efforts in 1971 is 2.2 percent more than the 17.8 percent of 10 years before. This is in spite of the fact that the congregations also have felt the pinch and faced tough, new alternatives. In the study, their anxieties and heightened local concern showed up in a call for more inclusive participation in determining church allocations, but not in revolt against them. Simply wanting more

[3] Annual meeting, United Methodist Board of Education, Nashville, Tenn., Jan. 24, 1972.
[4] Address, Board of Directors, United Church of Christ Board of Homeland Ministries, Bismarck, N. D., April 24, 1972.

voice in the process is a bird of a distinctly different color from challenging the basic thrust of denominational efforts, which would seem to present a much graver dilemma of principle. It did not, however, make a substantial showing. The main problem, as indicated by the data, seemed to lie elsewhere in a complex profusion of socio-economic forces, some not specifically related to the church itself.

Yet they crucially affect it and the study sought to uncover them, sort them out and explore possible remedies. Just what is happening to the religiously altruistic impulses of the people? Were they actually giving less? Why? What were the main reasons for not giving? For giving? Has there been some basic change in motivation? Are denominational materials designed to interpret and promote church programs missing the mark? Were members disillusioned with the way church funds are being raised or used?

Answers to these questions are of vital significance to the future of church operations, their direction, advance planning and scope. Most directly concerned with the specifics of the problem are the denominational departments assigned with the special task of cultivating church giving. These departments seek to guide and improve fund-raising approaches and also usually must deal with annual budget underwriting, long-term resource development through wills and legacies and with deepening awareness of the theological imperatives for material support of the church. Since the effectiveness of these departments depends on evoking responses among members, the job can't be done well without coming to grips with their present disposition. But what is it? That was the puzzle, the unknown first prerequisite. It is what this study sought to discover.

To begin with, American Protestants say they are giving more, not less, to the churches. Overall, fewer than 10 percent reduced their contributions in the last three years, while more than half increased them. The rest said they continued giving at about the same level. The greater financial support was particularly pronounced among the clergy of whom more than 80 percent in the United States and close to that in Canada upped their contributions. The figures are shown in Table 24.

This pattern is borne out by national statistics that show a continuing though slowing upward trend in total church receipts. However, the national figures also substantiate the tightening squeeze on church budgets at all levels. While giving has risen 13.5 percent in three years, inflation has boosted costs a total of 16 percent, making for a widening gap between the

table 24*

**CHANGES IN GIVING TO LOCAL CHURCH
LAST THREE YEARS**

Has your giving to the local church increased, decreased or remained about the same during the past three years?

	increased	decreased	about the same	no response
U. S. Laity	53.1	8.6	35.4	2.9
U. S. Pastors	83.4	3.5	12.4	.7
Canada Laity	45.6	11.9	38	4.5
Canada Pastors	76.5	2.1	21.4	0

* figures in percentages

churches' income and their ability to maintain their customary operations. In contrast, American spending for other purposes in the same period outran the pace of inflation—up 35 percent for recreation, up 36 percent for housing, up 57 percent for medical care.[5] In other words, elements other than inflation were affecting finances of the church. It lost ground economically in the inflationary weather while other fields kept surging ahead.

The particular problem clearly stemmed from other conditions. What were they? From various phases of the study, the focus became sharper as one after another of the ordinary scapegoats was toppled. Only a tiny fragment of the church constituency, six percent, has withheld contributions because of resentment at what their churches were doing, even though about half speculate that such a step might justifiably be taken, depending on the circumstances.

"It sounds good," joshed an Irene, South Dakota farmer, imagining the extra money he'd have as a result. "People should have the right to do it," said an Augusta, Kansas Baptist. "There's no point in giving to 'kunkletown'."

But the powerfully prevailing practice was against it. "We should be democratic and go along with decisions by the church at large," said a Jasper, Florida real estate dealer. Scattered voices did mention denominational stands about war, race, poverty, and civil disobedience as conceivable deterrents to giving, but just about as many cited such things as lavish buildings, waste, card parties and dancing, doctrinal shortcomings and lack of social consciousness. Actually, there was little concrete evidence of financial reprisals. "There are other methods of

[5] Op. cit., *Giving, USA.*

protest," said a Phoenix, Arizona Methodist, the wife of an attorney. "Nothing is all perfect," said a Burlington, Vermont business systems analyst. "You find things you like and dislike in everything."

Only a scanty minority—seven percent of the clergy and 16 percent of the laity—countenance the notion that a person should support the church only so long as its activities conform to his personal preferences. Most American church people, 88 percent of the clergy and 71 percent of the lay people, also feel their denominations should take definite stands on issues of social justice, using their influence to implement Christian ethics in society at large. Members strongly reject, upwards of 85 percent of them, the limiting of support only to undertakings which they themselves favor. "If you're going to be a Methodist, you should go with the Methodist Church," said a Jennings, Florida farmer.

Then where is the bottleneck? What siphons off resources, or what might augment them?

CONTROLS ON GIVING

In asking people why they had increased or decreased their contributions in the last three years, they also were asked to indicate reasons for the change. Here, some of the realities began to emerge. Most of them were distinctly "pragmatic" rather than "theological" in a sense either of religious commitment or propriety. A cogent element, life-style, a person's particular circumstances, his milieu and its pressures, showed up with mounting persistence as a key determinant.

A barber in Fargo, North Dakota, explaining his reduced giving, put it tersely, both cause and effect: "My earnings dropped with the trend to longer hair."

For the overwhelming proportion of those who had increased their giving, the blunt, simple reason was that they were making more money themselves. Similarly, the main reason for decreased giving was that their own paychecks or interest had declined. Among these depressive influences, only a wee fraction, 1.5 percent of U. S. lay people and 2.7 percent of those in Canada, said that church activity of which they had

table 25*

REASONS FOR CHANGES IN GIVING
What are some of the reasons for this change?

| | U.S. | | Canada | |
	Laity	Pastor	Laity	Pastor
more involved	6.2	.6	3.9	2.6
increased income	43.9	65.6	42.6	66.2
personal commitment	8.9	5.1	3.5	2.6
changed life situation	3	.6	3.1	0
church needs	8.7	4.7	20.7	11.7
increased income and other	15.1	19.3	6.6	14.3
less interest and income	8.2	2.6	13.7	2.6
disapprove church activity	1.5	.2	2.7	0
other	3.4	1.2	2.0	0
no response	1.1	0	1.2	0

* figures in percentages

disapproved had caused them to trim their donations. Table 25 shows the proportionate weight of various conditions in pushing gifts either up or down.

The same question was explored further in more impersonal terms, seeking to elicit underlying attitudes that people might not want to claim directly for themselves but which they nevertheless harbor. Instead of asking why they themselves had increased or decreased giving, they were asked to enumerate reasons why people generally do not give to their local church. Here again the reasons sensed most strongly had to do with deflecting family concerns, conditions and interests arising out of everyday situations, rather than denoting any specific backlash against the church. Yet, inferentially, the church is dealt a slight in relation to other concerns.

As people see it, the main thing blocking church support simply is a surpassing urge for more affluent living—for the "good things of life" that money can buy in the secular sphere apart from the church. This finding is in line with general economic indicators, showing that the sharp upsurge of spending in other fields has more than doubled the rate of growth in support for the church. Rival attractions seem to be gaining more of the religious dollar. This suggests that the roots of church financial difficulties, at least in part, go far deeper than surface gusts about passing policies or programs, reflecting a shifting scale of values that tends to upgrade other interests more markedly over the needs of the church.

The tug-of-war here, between personal acquisition of goods and the sharing of them for religious purposes, is as old as Christianity itself, but it also is continuously basic. Indications, both in the general national statistics and in this study, are that more of the church's financial moorings are being eroded by the pull of other desires. This puts the problem into the central zone of church teaching about the relative importance of faith and momentary satisfactions. It lifts a shadow over the comparative standing of the church in our time.

Yet no clue can be taken by itself as final and the study also brought out counterbalancing evidences of the church's enduring appeal among Americans, their esteem for it and high expectations of it. Furthermore, in citing reasons for not supporting it, they may have tended to pick the familiar, age-old lure of "good things" in the world as the main obstacle simply because of its familiarity. Other next most highly rated reasons, however, displayed the impact of sheer practical considerations—emergency demands of illness or extra family burdens and the vagaries of wages and job. Table 26 shows the percentage of respondents ranking each of the reasons in the first six places. The highest total of 83.2 percent of them included in that upper bracket the overriding concern for "good things" as the main influence cutting off support for the church. It also was placed first by the biggest proportion of people.

The breakdown by countries and between clergy and laity also indicates a corresponding picture, as shown in Table 27. The urge for the "good things" apart from the church comes first in shutting off gifts to it, followed by extraordinary family responsibilities and the fiscal vicissitudes of income and employment.

Obviously clergymen are not buffeted by unemployment as much as the laity, indicating the clergy's more sheltered economic circumstances. Overall, the pastors put being thrown out of work at the bottom of the list, while ordinary

table 26*.

REASONS FOR NONSUPPORT OF THE CHURCH

Percentages of respondents ranking reasons for nonsupport of the church in the first six places among a total of 10.

	First	Second	Third	Fourth	Fifth	Sixth
Money used to provide the good things of life to family	31.5	14.2	11.0	9.1	9.2	8.2
Money used to meet extra family obligations (care of elderly, long term illness, etc.)	12.6	17.4	17.4	14.1	10.2	7.7
Irregular or unpredictable income	10.2	14.5	11.8	12.8	12.6	9.5
Unemployed	10.6	7.9	7.7	7.3	7.3	10.4
Money used for education	3.1	9.1	12.4	14.6	11.6	7.7
Give charitable money to nonchurch causes	5.6	8.3	10.7	11.2	12.0	12.2
Church not important in society	9.4	9.6	7.2	7.8	9.1	9.7
Church doesn't need more money	6.0	7.7	7.8	8.1	8.9	10.0
Dislike minister	4.7	4.7	5.4	5.7	6.4	8.5
Dislike church leaders	3.2	4.8	6.2	6.5	7.6	9.2

* figures in percentages

REASONS FOR NONSUPPORT OF THE LOCAL CHURCH
table 27*

What would you say are the most important reasons why people do not give to their local church?

	U.S.		Average Laity	Canada Involved Laity	Clergy
	Laity	Clergy			
Money used to provide the good things of life to family.	1	1	1	1	1
Money used to meet extra family obligations (care of elderly, father, mother, long-term illness, etc.).	2	2	2	3	4
Irregular or unpredictable income	3	4	4	4	3
Money used for education	4	6	7	7	6
Unemployed	5	10	5	8	9
Give charitable money to nonchurch causes	6	7	3	5	7
The church is not important in society.	7	3	6	2	2
Church doesn't need more money	8	5	8	6	5
Dislike minister	9	9	9	10	8
Dislike church leaders	10	8	10	9	10

* Figures show rankings, 1 to 10, in order of importance. Weighted scoring was used in the Canadian calculations, with each respondent's answer weighted in accordance with the overall proportion of people in his size and type of church.

members ranked it in the upper half of conditions barring church contributions. Furthermore, U.S. lay people find the costs of educating their young take a heavier toll than they do for the clergy or for Canadians generally. This is understandable since other phases of the study showed that the U.S. laity includes a higher proportion of college graduates than the Canadian membership, making for a U.S. environment in which the necessity for a college degree is more acute in the job market, thereby intensifying the burden of paying for higher education. This was especially the case in the populous northeastern part of the United States and for persons between 30 and 64 years old (in the educational years of their young). It also was more the case for whites than for blacks.

In the smaller congregations of less than 150 members, the unpredictable irregularity of income was more crucial in wiping out church support than extra family obligations, which took precedence in the larger churches and also generally. Members of the big congregations of more than 750 members also were less constrained by unemployment than were people of the medium-sized and small congregations, many of them in rural areas where uncertainties of income were considered more disabling.

Contradicting past surmises about it, few think that church giving is curbed by antagonisms either to church leadership or to ministers. In fact, these were rated the least of causes by ordinary lay people. Strangely, blacks were more inclined than whites to regard resentment at church leadership as a roadblock, even though the generally expressed impression has been that backlash at church leadership was sharpest among whites. The data, however, dispute it. On the whole, negative attitudes toward church leadership simply were brushed aside by American lay people as being of little consequence.

The chief reason for not contributing, as those who were asked see it, is simply that old spellbinder—the yen for the materially "good things of life" coupled with unusual family obligations and their own financial situations.

However, one of the most haunting notes is that pastors are much more prone than the membership-at-large (with the exception of the special, relatively small Canadian category of highly "involved laity") to see the problem as a decline in the church's importance. Lay people, as indicated both here and in other answers on why people quit church, emphatically do not go along with their pastors' idea that the church is losing significance in modern society. The difference on this point is consistently sharp throughout the study, implying that the clergy, those ordained and paid to uphold the church's credibility, tend to be more pessimistic about it than the church members. This seems an odd and disturbing disparity, perhaps adding to the much-discussed sagging morale among pastors and their reduced confidence in their work.

U. S. clergy consider a shrinking of the church's prestige as the third most critical factor in choking off support for it, while Canadian clergy consider it the second most important factor, more decisive than all the possible reasons except the enticements of "good things." In jarring contrast, most lay people don't detect any dimming of the church's luster as a major hindrance to its support. They put this implication far down the list, in sixth place among the average Canadian lay person and in seventh place among U.S. lay people.

Curiously however, the smaller congregations, those under 250 members, are more likely than the larger churches to go along with the clergy-men in their bleak estimate. This is in keeping with the small church tendency to see society as turning away from God and the church. But they still remain more sanguine about the church's strength than do the clergymen, and overall, American lay people take a brighter view of the church's continuing importance, de-spite their pastors' glumness about it.

Furthermore, clergy are much more apt than lay people to say that the reason for nonsupport of the church is that the "church doesn't need more money." Clergy rate this as the fifth most important basis for not giving, while ordinary lay members discount it to eighth place. In this case, they register a greater sensitivity than their pastors to the realities of the church's financial needs. The opposite would have seemed likelier, but here again we confront the hard data of the unexpected.

REASONS FOR GIVING

Another revealing peculiarity is that the rea-sons for not giving, in concentrating on the grati-fication of secular desires and the practical ex-igencies of job and income, differ in their very nature from the reasons affirmed for giving itself. In the latter case, instead of focusing on concrete financial considerations, the reasons cited for contributing to the church take on an intensely religious character. The question arises as to whether the positive religious intent or the negative practical considerations carry more weight regarding the extent of church support.

However, bypassing that issue for the mo-ment, Americans in explaining their motives for giving to the church in a positive way see them chiefly in theological dimensions. More than 80 percent of all respondents agreed that gifts to the church are an expression of their faith, as shown in Table 28. Even a bigger proportion of clergy, 95 percent of them, agreed with this appraisal of the matter as religiously based. Lay people didn't ratify the reverential aspect in such wholesale fashion, suggesting either a more critical or less theologically discerning attitude.

table 28*

GIVING MONEY TO THE CHURCH IS AN EXPRESSION OF A PERSON'S FAITH

	All Respondents (3447)	Canada		U.S.	
		Clergy	Laity	Clergy	Laity
Strongly Agree	31.5	45.8	17.0	49.8	28.6
Agree	36.1	26.7	29.8	34.5	36.9
Tend to Agree	12.6	15.5	19.1	11.3	12.4
Tend to Disagree	6.9	6.5	9.0	3.2	7.8
Disagree	10.4	5.2	19.1	0.9	11.4
Strongly Disagree	2.4	0.3	5.1	0.2	2.7
No Response	0.1	0	0.8	0.2	0.1

* figures in percentages

Nevertheless, most church members felt that money and faith have a direct relationship. They feel this more strongly in smaller churches, those under 300 members, and in non-metropolitan areas than they do in the larger and metropolitan churches. This suggests that the smaller, non-metropolitan churches are most closely attuned with the clergy's highly religious concept of the roots of giving.

Across the board, however, the theological rationale predominates when people cite the specific positive reasons for contributing to the church, shown in Chart 4, page 128. "Gratitude to God" is the most pervasively cited motivation, followed by the convictions that "giving is a part of worship," that it is "a privilege to share," that it is done out of "love for others," and in fifth place, that it is "an obligation placed on man by God." Rated next in line, in an intermediate zone, were the lesser personal and practical considerations—a recognition that the church needs money, a view that giving it is a "duty of membership," a sense of being "proud of our church," an approval of its programs and feeling good about supporting it.

Far down the list, in the bottom rankings, were the factors customarily regarded as paramount—habit, guilt, fear, social pressure and desire to gain God's favor. These traditionally assumed motives, widely if subtly used in trying to promote contributions, were sharply downgraded by members, suggesting either that such approaches have been wrong in the past or have become so, that members have cast off the suppliant anxieties about it and become more positively intentioned in their giving. They say they do it freely in gratitude, worship and as a privilege, and not out of any submission to pressure or to ease their consciences.

"Our giving is in response to all God has given us," said a Sunset Hills, Missouri engineer. "It means helping God's work," said the wife of a Lebanon, Tennessee service station manager. "It's out of love for Christ," said an Ashland,

CHART 4

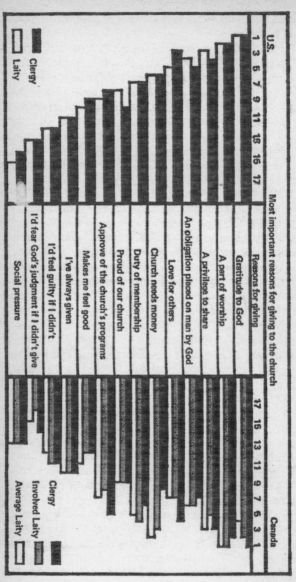

Most important reasons for giving to the church

Reasons for giving	U.S.	Canada
Gratitude to God		
A part of worship		
A privilege to share		
An obligation placed on man by God		
Love for others		
Church needs money		
Duty of membership		
Proud of our church		
Approve of the church's programs		
Makes me feel good		
I've always given		
I'd feel guilty if I didn't		
I'd fear God's judgment if I didn't give		
Social pressure		

U.S.: 1 3 5 7 9 11 13 15 17
Clergy / Laity

Canada: 17 15 13 11 9 7 5 3 1
Clergy / Involved Laity / Average Laity

Massachusetts housewife. "You give because you want to."

This open-hearted assessment of it, and the rejection of the guilt-salving pressure motives, offers a clear-cut pointer that guidance materials on the subject should be kept in a positive vein if they are to strike an affirmative chord in most members.

Aside from their generally unconstrained impulses in giving, however, an intangibly, recurring difference appears in attitudes toward the church between laity in the two countries. Canadians, reflecting their characteristically stronger regard for the church as a structured institution, put more emphasis on financial support as a part of worship, as a necessity to the church and as a duty than do the U.S. lay people. They, in turn, stress their own gratitude to God, their fulfilling of an obligation to Him and love for others, all personally grounded impulses rather than being centered on an institution, as is the case with the Canadians.

For both Canadian and U.S. lay people, however, the specific approval of the church's program is far down the list as a spur to giving, in seventh place among the average Canadians, eighth place for "involved" Canadians and ninth for U.S. laity. Clergy in both countries rate it a notch higher indicating that a sanctioning appraisal of the church's program is not quite as influential among members in affecting their contributions as the clergy think it is.

On the whole, the heavy concentration on religious-theological motivations stands out clearly in Table 29, page 130, showing the percentages of upper rankings, from one to six, given each of the 16 factors.

Only small, scattered variations are brought out in the classification of responses by church

table 29*

RESPONDENTS RANKING REASONS FOR GIVING IN FIRST SIX PLACES

	First	Second	Third	Fourth	Fifth	Sixth
Gratitude to God	45.5	12.2	7.4	4.6	3.7	3.0
Giving is a part of worship	12.6	20.3	17.6	13.6	9.5	6.0
It's a privilege to share	5.8	13.1	17.0	17.6	12.0	7.5
Giving is an obligation placed on man by God	10.4	10.7	7.7	6.5	8.0	5.9
Love for others	3.8	14.0	13.7	12.6	8.9	5.5
The church needs money	7.0	6.1	7.7	9.7	12.2	16.1
It's a duty of membership	4.3	7.5	8.1	10.0	11.0	10.9
I'm proud of our church	2.8	3.6	5.0	6.0	7.4	7.4
I approve of the church's programs	1.9	3.7	4.8	7.5	10.8	10.9
It makes me feel good	1.1	2.5	3.5	4.2	5.6	7.9
I've always given	1.3	1.6	2.1	2.4	3.5	5.9
I'd feel guilty if I didn't	0.6	1.2	1.4	1.4	2.5	5.9
I'd fear God's judgment if I didn't	0.2	0.4	0.5	0.3	0.4	0.9
Social pressure of friends and/or associates	0.1	0.1	0.1	0.2	0.2	0.5
I want to get God's favor	0.1	0.3	0.4	0.3	0.4	0.6
Person next to me at worship gave	0.1	0.1	0.0	0.0	0.3	0.2

* figures in percentages

size, as shown in Table 30, page 132. For larger churches, those of 250 or more members, "approval of the church's program" is slightly more important in stimulating giving than for the smaller congregations, although still quite minimal and subordinate. But it does hint at the somewhat more judgmental pragmatism among the larger, less intimate parishes. For the smaller groups, being "proud of our church" rates a bit higher than it does for the big congregations, disclosing again that thread of beleaguered defensiveness that seems to crop up regularly among smaller churches.

Classification by age also displays some minor but typical differences. Those of tenderer years, under 30, express a more unreserved inclusive human affection in their reasons for giving, ranking "love for others" as the fourth most persuasive factor, putting them close to the high human idealism of the clergy, who rate that influence as third. However, by the ages of 30 to 64, lay people have become more dubious of that indiscriminately loving urge, putting it down in fifth place, while the time-seasoned older folk of 65 or more put it in seventh place, sharply minimizing it.

Younger lay people under 30, exhibiting their usual independence from old-style compulsions, also are less disposed to give as "an obligation," discounting that factor to sixth or eighth place in the two countries, while older persons rated it more strongly in fourth place. However, lay people generally assert a sort of hardboiled pragmatism about giving, ranking both obligation and need of the church for money higher than do the clergy. The clergy, resembling the young in their humanitarianism, give greater importance to "love for others" than do lay people.

Nevertheless, all of these variables become

table 30*

RANKINGS OF MOST IMPORTANT REASONS FOR GIVING BY SIZE OF CHURCH

	less than 150	150-249	250-299	300-499	500-749	750-1,499	1,500+
Gratitude to God	1	1	1	1	1	1	1
Giving is a part of worship	2	2	2	2	2	2	2
It's a privilege to share	3	3	3	3	3	3	3
Love for others	4	4	5	4	4	4	5
Obligation placed on man by God	5	5	6	5	6	6	4
Church needs money	6	6	7	6	5	5	7
It's a duty of membership	7	7	4	7	7	7	6
Proud of church	8	8	9	9	9	9	9
Approve of church's programs	9	9	8	8	8	8	8

• Based on mean scores of all respondents.

only a faint counterpoint to a central theme that sounds forth strongly again as the questions about giving narrow down to specific, personal determinants. While church members dwelt mainly on lofty theological-religious promptings in assessing motives for giving in broad generalities, they took a quite different tack when asked, in directly individual terms, "What are the most important influences on you as you decide how much money to give to your local church?"

Here once more, the practical considerations returned to the forefront. By far, "income" stood out as the most prominently mentioned factor, followed by another practical yardstick, the "needs of the church." As shown in Table 31, page 134, "biblical teachings" drew the next most first-place ratings, but much fewer than either of the two utilitarian influences. It also received a smaller total percentage in the upper six places, altogether about nine percent less than those citing "family obligations" in that upper range.

The main point is that when members were asked about the specific factors controlling their own giving, practical conditions again became dominant, just as was the case in reactions to why people don't give. Unlike the generalized, impersonal grading of motives, which waxed highly theological, the tune changes to a more practical key when the issue becomes personal.

As in other instances, lesser subthemes also emerge in the breakdowns into various categories. Smaller churches, once more displaying their organizational protectiveness, put "needs of the church" ahead even of individual income, reversing the order of other groups. Members of smaller churches also report being more moved by biblical teachings than do the larger congregations. Persons over 40 also consider scriptural injunctions more compelling in gauging their

table 31

REASONS FOR HOW MUCH TO GIVE

What are the most important influences on you as you decide how much money to give to your local church?

(Percentages of respondents ranking factors in first six places)

	First	Second	Third	Fourth	Fifth	Sixth
Income	31.1	18.4	13.7	10.1	8.4	5.6
The needs of the church	17.0	21.8	20.7	14.9	9.7	6.1
Biblical teachings	19.1	9.5	8.8	8.6	7.3	7.9
Amount left after meeting family obligations	8.0	14.8	11.5	11.3	11.9	12.2
Frequency of participation in church activities	10.1	10.8	13.0	14.8	14.4	11.2
Guidelines given by church	4.4	8.8	11.6.	13.6	13.0	11.5
Feelings at moment of giving	2.8	5.6	7.9	10.0	12.7	14.4
Give same amount each year	4.6	6.1	6.9	8.0	9.1	12.2
Presentation of visitors	0.9	1.5	2.1	3.2	4.4	5.9
Contributions of friends	0.4	1.2.	1.2	1.7	2.9	4.4

contributions than do younger persons. Members under 40, those in the stage of heavy family-rearing expenses, regard family obligations as more decisive than older people in determining what's left over for church support. Here again, varying concrete circumstances stamp their mark.

AMOUNTS GIVEN

Reinforcing the evidence that everyday secular concerns become preeminent in the actual

table 32

**AMOUNTS FROM CLERGY AND LAITY
TO THE CHURCH IN 1970**

Percentages of laity and clergy contributing various amounts to the church in 1970.

	United Church of Canada			U.S.	
	Clergy	Involved Laity	Average Laity	Clergy	Laity
none	0	0	13.8	1.1	7.5
less than $ 50	0	0	12.8	0.7	9.6
$ 50-$ 99	0.4	0	16.9	0.7	9.2
$100-$199	10.0	3.7	26.8	2.1	16.6
$200-$299	13.7	18.8	12.0	3.7	12.5
$300-$399	37.0	9.8	7.1	6.0	10.5
$400-$499	7.3	13.6	2.8	7.1	7.3
$500 or more	31.6	54.0	7.8	78.5	26.8
Median for week				$14.65	$ 5.52

giving patterns among lay people were the findings about just how much the respondents contributed. Obviously, from the data shown on giving in Table 32 and on income in Table 33, it is not just income alone nor the laity's generalized devotional affirmations that most forcefully regulate the real amounts they give, but rather other surrounding forces impinging on their

table 33*

TOTAL FAMILY INCOME IN 1970

| | Canada | | | U.S. | |
	Clergy	Involved Laity	Average Laity	Clergy	Laity
no response	0	4.7	6.1	2.1	5.2
less than $ 3,000	0	1.2	9.8	0.7	7.6
$ 3,000-$ 4,999	0	0.8	7.2	1.4	7.7
$ 5,000-$ 6,999	23.9	8.1	7.9	11.7	9.2
$ 7,000-$ 9,999	32.1	10.0	17.9	33.9	16.0
$10,000-$13,999	14.2	18.9	20.8	31.6	25.3
$14,000-$17,999	29.6	17.3	13.8	12.2	15.0
$18,000-$24,999	0.2	10.0	10.9	6.2	8.8
$25,000 or more	0	29.0	5.5	0.2	5.1
Median for year				$10,111	$11,075

* figures in table show percentages of respondents reporting varying income levels.

lives, including the drive they cited as the chief hindrance to church giving—the pouring of their resources into shoring up family status.

The impact of these diffused influences stands out vividly in the fact that clergymen, who on the average are paid less than lay people, contributed nearly three times more than they do. A clergyman in the United States earns a median salary of $10,111 annually compared to the $11,075 earned by an average lay person, but the minister donates a median $14.65 a week to the church, compared to the $5.52 given by the lay member. Contributions of ordinary Canadian members also are sharply less than gifts by the clergy. Only the much higher paid "involved laity" in Canada excel their pastors in giving. As shown in Table 34, page 138, lay people in every age group above 20 earn more than clergymen, but the clergymen give far more to the church.

What does this mean? Two implications can be drawn. One is that clergymen, who usually are provided with housing and its upkeep in addition to their salaries, are thereby cushioned against these drains on their income, leaving them with more financial latitude to support the church. However, many studies over the years have consistently confirmed the substandard salaries of ministers, including their housing allotments, in relation to other professions. This, coupled with the exceedingly sharp difference between their giving and that of lay people, suggests there must be other factors at work.

This points to the alternative interpretation that lay people must be under greater pressure, whatever its nature, to channel a much bigger share of their income into purposes other than religion. It could be heavier family obligations, although there are no readily available explanations why this might be so. What appears more

table 34*

FAMILY INCOME BY AGE

Annual Income	Clergy					Laity					
	20-29	30-39	40-49	50-64	65+	14-19	20-29	30-39	40-49	50-64	65+
Less than $3,000	3.7	0	0	0.5	4.9	7.5	5.0	1.3	0.4	7.0	25.2
$ 3,000 – 4,999	3.7	1.4	0.6	1.6	2.4	2.9	8.6	1.3	2.4	7.4	22.8
$ 5,000 – 6,999	37.0	19.0	5.4	5.3	22.0	4.0	15.5	5.8	5.8	9.1	16.5
$ 7,000 – 9,999	44.4	29.9	30.9	22.0	12.2	6.4	24.5	18.1	14.3	20.1	11.7
$10,000 – 13,999	11.1	21.8	39.5	37.8	22.0	21.4	28.2	36.4	32.5	23.7	8.5
$14,000 – 17,999	0	7.0	18.6	13.8	4.9	8.7	7.7	20.9	22.5	13.9	5.3
$18,000 – 24,999	0	3.5	5.4	8.5	9.8	13.3	5.0	9.4	11.6	9.3	2.2
$25,000 and over	0	0	0.6	0	0	8.7	3.2	4.8	7.4	6.0	1.5
no response	0	0	0	1.6	22.0	27.2	2.3	2.0	3.0	3.6	6.3

* Figures in table show percentages in each age category receiving various levels of income — data for the United States only.

138

likely is that even though lay people generalize just as graphically about their religious motivations for giving as the clergy, lay members are not nearly as consistent in translating that devotion into concrete terms of dollars and cents. The abstractly expressed ideals aren't matched by tangible investment in the cause.

Basically it is a question of putting beliefs into action in the kind of medium of exchange by which this world functions, in the operational currency that gets the work done, turns the wheels and keeps any enterprise going. The more theologically versed clergy see the immediate tie between espousing faith in principle and backing it through receipts of their labor, a connection that lay people don't seem to grasp so fully. At least they don't act on it.

WILLS AND DEFERRED GIVING

The differing tendencies in regard to giving to the church are further substantiated by the handling of wills to be executed at death, and through deferred giving plans that have become increasingly available through annuities and lifetime estates. In Canada where laws make wills more necessary, 94 percent of the clergy, 91 percent of the involved laity and 70 percent of the average laity have made wills. In the United States, only 56 percent of the clergy and 44 percent of the laity have done so, although the proportion increases with age to upwards of 70 percent in the 60s and beyond. As shown in Table 35, more than twice as many Canadian pastors than lay members and nearly two-thirds more U.S. pastors than lay members have included bequests to the church in their wills.

Clergymen also were more likely to name a denominational or churchwide agency as the benefactors than were lay people, who were more apt to name a local church as the recipient. When those who had not included the church in their wills were asked why, clergymen tended to cite specific reasons, such as special family obligations or feelings that each contemporary generation should support the church of its time without dependence on ancestral forebears. On the other hand, the most common response of lay people was that it hadn't occurred to them.

table 35*

BEQUESTS TO THE CHURCH
Have you included a bequest to the church in your will?

	yes	no	no response
U.S.			
Clergy	25.8	73.6	0.6
Laity	15.0	84.6	0.4
Canada			
Clergy	25.5	74.5	
Involved Laity	9.3	90.7	
Average Laity	9.8	90.2	

* figures in percentages

PSYCHOLOGICAL NOTE

A young boy pops his belt at his mother's favorite vase and it crashes to the floor. "Why did you do it?" she demands. "I don't know." "But you must know." "I don't." Despite the parental frustrations, the boy probably is just as bewildered. He doesn't know.

A lot of behavior is like that, startling, puzzling, inexplicable. The same submerged, indefinable impulses affect giving in the church. For instance, it has been found that some rather generous contributors put a ceiling on their gifts, even though financially able to give more, so they won't be regarded as trying to usurp control of the church.[6]

Apart from individual idiosyncracies, however, the precise interests and urges that enter into church support cannot be nailed down solely to objectives and principles alone, no matter how strongly they are affirmed. Beyond these overevaluations, we face the strange complexity of the human personality itself. Psychologists say we are driven both by "push qualities," the innate drives within us, and by "sentiments" or "rational choices," the positions we take mostly as a result of surrounding influences in which we develop and live.

Although we may not like to think so, we are creatures of our climate. Our behavior is partly determined, emotionally, occupationally, socially and economically, by our group associations. It is this element that bobbed up recurringly in the present study as a compelling aspect of attitudes toward the church and behavior in it. Life-styles, the cultural environment, age and socio-economic circumstances in which people live, emerge as a strong force in their conduct.

For example, older people with the longest records of commitment to the church and the most fixed convictions about its doctrines and rôle, were more inclined to select habit, guilt, fear and social pressure as reasons for giving than was the predominant, coming population of

[6] *Giving to Churches: A Sociological Study of Eight Catholic and Lutheran Churches*, Kenneth G. Lutterman, Ph.D. thesis, University of Wisconsin, 1962.

younger people between 30 and 50. They saw their support of the church in freer, more positive and purposeful terms, reflecting a style and changing outlook on life that foretokens a new day and basically cheerier way for the church.

Nevertheless, many of them cited attractive options outside the church as reasons for leaving it and the hankering for "good things" as reason for not supporting it. But their responses made plain that they were not belittling the church, only saying that it needs a keener dedication to its purposes. Chiefly, they wanted more concentrated attention to teaching, to expounding the basic tenets of faith.

"The lack of biblical preaching is a main trouble," said a Jackson, Kentucky school teacher. "Naturally we need to relate our faith to the problems of today, but people are looking for the inner certainties to give them the strength to do it. What we're hearing is more of a situational theology that doesn't appeal to a lot of people or help them. They're looking for something that says, 'This is the way,' not 'Your opinion is as good as mine'."

The plea came not just from old-timers, jolted by modernity, but rather from the whole spectrum of membership, including the young. At the same time, most of them also upheld the church's social responsibilities. But when it comes to financial contributions, their stated motivations don't always jibe with the actual behavior.

To test this factor, the data from the U.S. laity was subjected to computer analysis. The results showed that giving had a strong correlation to pragmatic circumstances, the number of dependents, income, length of membership, education, age, but very little with expressed convictions or the declared reasons for giving. The implications were that economic standards and concerns, the extent of a person's church activity, his past pattern of giving, his social-educational milieu and the amounts given by friends had more to do with his level of church support than his stated motives for it.

The tests dramatize not so much the difference between saying and doing as the power of the group, the impress of community attitudes, values and understandings. People want to respond, want to believe, want to act and to help, but the findings show they need the supportive interests of their peers and a more explicit warranty for it in order to do so in keeping with their ideals.

CONCLUSIONS

"Where your treasure is," Jesus said, "there will your heart be also." [7]

That laconic, lancing insight sums up the basic interwoven nature of our lives, body and spirit, earthly environment and deepest aspiration, bound together, interacting, unified, the highest commitments expressed in the commonest material ways. This intertwined web of pragmatic situations and highest loyalties has stood forth unmistakably in this study, a constant, interfusing composite of lofty motives and expedient circumstances, of noble intents and circumscribing environments, an intermingled confluence of urges and influences that meld and blend in indistinguishable combination. We are a mix, flesh and soul, a psychosomatic whole, integral beings both of dreams and dust. Yet Jesus said the highest values always find expression in the commonest material ways.

That fundamentally materialistic script of our

[7] Matthew 6:21

lives, even in expressing the loftiest visions, was manifested by Jesus himself through his physical incarnation of Godliness in the clay and coinage of the world itself. When he offered his pungent observation about the true measure of reality for human beings, he pinned down the inseparable link between a person's spiritual values and the uses to which he puts the tangible proceeds of his own labors. The saying has been an old standby in efforts to sustain support of the church, but the findings of this study raise serious questions about whether lay people generally actively subscribe to it.

The fact remains, however, that we are material creatures and we express ourselves in material ways. Our skill and sweat is exacted and projected through the monetary medium; it is the fruit of our daily labors. Wages, not the crops of old, are the substance of our work. Our uses of that medium, this yield of our energies, defines how we use ourselves. It is the index of our lives, the food on our tables, the roof overhead, the rights or wrongs we underwrite and perpetuate. Jesus singled out this down-to-earth realism in his pithy epigram.

As the study brings out, however, lay people don't demonstrate an active congruity between their high religious attestations about giving and their substantive participation in it. They firmly declare the high motivations, but the enactment of them in concrete terms pales in comparison. In any case, the typical contribution of Americans to the church doesn't seem to mesh with their strong avowals of dedication to it.

This implies a question, not of the laity's asserted devotion to the church, but of their theological competency and application, which, in turn, throws the spotlight on the caliber of teaching in the church about giving, a ministerial function. As the findings show, lay people regard seeking the "good things" apart from religion as the chief detraction siphoning off support from it, indicating some pervasive inadequacy in realizing the interlocking claims of faith on workaday, secular life and its produce. The results suggest that people see these two spheres virtually in opposition rather than in combination, almost as two unrelated realms, tugging competitively at them.

Their assessment of barriers to giving appear to conform more with their actual giving than do their asserted highly devotional reasons for it. In short, the negative side of the analysis seems to tell more about the real problem than do the appraisals from a positive point of view.

Certainly general economic trends, high costs of living, a tight employment market and other difficulties hurt the church's finances, but not necessarily any more than it affects other areas of life. Yet the overall indications are that in the squeeze at the turn of the seventies, the church felt it more keenly than most other concerns, indicating some particular distress in the churches.

The findings turn up little evidence that the church's social stance or its doctrinal issues have lessened loyalty to it or crimped support of it. To the contrary, people equate their highest aspirations, gratitude to God and worship itself, with support for the church.

The problem thus must lie elsewhere and the clue that fits most logically with other findings appears to come in the consensus that the appeal of "good things" beyond the church acts as the chief drag on support for it. Only old folks, those over 64, and teen-agers, that new generation with its conscience honed to a fine edge in confronting the culture's jaded affluence and rawly exposed social ills, refused to see the magnetism of secular "good things" as a prime cause under-cutting church support. To them, the prosperously accoutered status didn't look that tantalizing. But others saw it as the main financial rival to the church.

Although in their generalizations about giving, they registered high religious commitment, their emphasis on the enticements of other "good things" as a main deterrent indicates their view of a basic dichotomy between religious and material concerns. This also is mirrored further in the chasm between their stated high idealism about giving and its meagerness in actuality. The difficulty thus seems lodged not in new conditions but in an old distortion that divides, fragments and compartmentalizes life itself, a distortion that perhaps has been heightened in the modern age by technology's tendency to cut off mankind from its moorings in the grace of creation itself.

The old split, inherited mostly from Platonic thought, has been a chronic problem throughout Judeo-Christian history, continually tending to divorce religious life from the earth-borne realities of existence. In the scriptural perspective, the two spheres don't develop separately but together in mutual interaction, and it is this lesson that seems to have become obscure in the church's tutelage.

Clergymen, through their special training, reject the false rupturing of life into segments, and in consequence, they display a greater harmony between their expressed religious motivations and their habits of church support. The laity, however, show less consistency. They also are generally less grounded in theological understanding. Since this is a major distinction in their background from that of the clergy, it may also be a source of the differences in their giving.

That would situate the nub of the problem at a basic point of church and clergy responsibility—the duty to teach more adequately the truth of our faith, that it is wrought of the stuff of this earth, flesh of our flesh, funds of our fortunes, whether slim or sleek.

5.

terms, teachings
and techniques

It's an old word, plucked from the Bible and kicking around in sermons and ecclesiastical collection-boosting circles for years. It's a solid, clean word, drawn from the ancient rural world of pure air, stately manor houses and green rolling fields. It has none of the taint of "filthy lucre" about it and would seem to appeal to the noble, dutiful instincts of most people. It has connotations of landed estates, of lordly owners and faithful servants, a kind of feudal majesty.

The word is "stewardship" and it has been the trusty label long used by the churches in teaching members about responsibilities for contributing a rightful share of their substance to the church. The trouble is, for all of the word's richly laden ramifications, most people don't know its normally intended meaning.

In this study, they were asked to define it and the answers wandered the gamut of speculation. A few samples: "It's being like one of Christ's disciples." "It's living nearly as right as we can." "It's being a waiter." "I should know but I've forgotten." "It's giving testimony." "It beats me."

Some, however, more accurately phrased the traditional meaning. "It's accounting to God for the talents and gifts he has given us." "It's giving back to God a portion of what he has given you."

Strictly speaking, stewardship means managing another's property, affairs or the household-hotel of a large estate, or in a limited sense, handling provisions of passengers on shipboard. Ecologists have come to use it in regard to taking care of nature itself, the "stewardship of the earth." In a religious context, as used by church stewardship program developers, it means serving as God's steward in the world he created, caring for it and being accountable to him for the benefits reaped from it.

"Every one to whom much is given, of him will much be required," Jesus said in describing a master's expectations of a faithful steward.[1] As St. Paul put it, "It is required of stewards that they be found trustworthy." [2]

In short, in customary church terminology, it means exercising time, talent and treasure in fidelity to the Creator who bestowed them on us.

Only a minority of lay people understood the concept in this way—42 percent of the U.S. laity, 45 percent of the "involved" Canadian laity and 26 percent of the average Canadian laity. In contrast, 84 percent of the clergy in both countries handily set down the standard phraseology about use of "time, talent and treasure" in fealty to God. They knew the institutional jargon, but most people in the church today didn't.

This majority offered a variety of answers, most of them seeing stewardship as activity directed toward other people, such as rendering help, service, witnessing to the Gospel or working together. Such definitions came from only 11 percent of the clergy, but from 40 percent of the U.S. laity, 51 percent of the average Canadian laity and 29 percent of the "involved" Canadians. To them, stewardship basically denoted useful activity, the exertions of themselves in reli-

[1] Luke 12:48
[2] 1st Corinthians 4:2

giously productive ways. While this is part of the classic concept, it is without the core implication of applying human potentialities in responsibility to the Creator who provided them and to whom they inherently belong.

Most of the other respondents—altogether about 19 percent of the laity and four percent of the clergy—either put the focus on money, assorted other ideas, or said they didn't know.

table 36*

MEANING OF STEWARDSHIP

Would you please tell me what you mean by stewardship?

| | Canadian | | | U.S. | |
	Clergy	Involved Laity	Average Laity	Clergy	Laity
no response/ don't know	3.8	10.7	16.7	1.6	9.6
involves use or sharing time, talent, resources	83.7	45.4	26.0	85.2	41.6
focus on money	1.1	14.0	4.8	2.5	7.4
witness and service	7.6	23.3	39.2	9.9	30.9
helping others	0.4	3.0	3.8	0.5	5.1
working together	0	2.8	8.0	0	3.6
other	3.4	0.7	1.5	0.3	1.8

* figures in percentages

Classifications into age categories showed some marked differences. A particularly large number of lay people under 30 years of age, a fourth of them, simply said they didn't know, compared to only a tenth of those over that age in the United States. The older people were much more inclined to take a stab at it, even if not precisely on target. Younger clergy, those under 30, were more likely than their older colleagues to see the word in active terms of expanding the Gospel and service instead of in the traditional broader sense of accounting responsibly for all of life's endowments in respect to their source in God.

In sum, the customary official term used to build financial support for the church has only vague or indirect reference to that cause in the minds of most lay people. They and the younger clergy tend to think of it in terms of varied activity rather than a total orientation of the substance of life.

Somehow, church terminology on the point has misfired or lost vividness in an age when few have known "stewards" of the palace or of an agricultural domain. The historic term has a dated vintage about it, implying that possibly some of the program that goes with it may be suffering from similar decrepitude.

THE TITHE

The variety of materials developed to help inform and persuade people to give to the church have been built on a series of assumptions, both theological and practical. The basic theological assumption is that the central norm for giving is prescribed in Scripture—the tithe, 10 percent of a person's income. The rationale for this norm is based on the stewardship concept, that human beings are keepers of possessions with which God has entrusted them for a period of time and that in gratitude for it, they should return a share of its yield in direct proportion to the total received, a tenth.

"All the tithe of the land, whether the seed of the land or the fruit of the trees, is the Lord's," says Leviticus 27:30. "It is holy to the Lord."

The word tithe, itself, comes from the Hebrew "maaser," meaning one-tenth.

However, the idea runs into some complicated sledding in the economically labyrinthine modern society in which we now live, with income taxes taking off a first big bite and other chunks going into schools, community chests and many government welfare services that once had been the province of religion in the theocratic society in which the tithe was formulated. As a result, various modifications have arisen. Some churches recommend what they call the "modern tithe," five percent to the church, five percent to other charities—both after taxes. Others simply teach "proportionate giving," meaning a fixed share in relation to income. Nevertheless, the old norm remains, a proverbial guide in regard to church giving.

It is no longer, however, considered a minimum denominational standard by the bulk either of clergymen or lay people. The traditional view of it as a minimum standard is upheld in the United States by only 27 percent of the laity and 20 percent of the pastors, and in Canada, by only 10 percent of the laity and six percent of the clergy. More than 75 percent of the clergy and about 53 percent of the laity in both countries see the tithe as only one suggestion among many about proportionate giving, as shown in Table 37.

A comparatively large percentage of Canadians, 17 percent of the clergy, 13 percent of the involved laity and seven percent of the average laity, said the tithe simply was no longer important or useful. In the United States, however, only three percent of the laity and one percent of the clergy took that position. A much bigger bloc of laity in both countries, 33 percent of the ordinary Canadian laymen, 16 percent of the "in-

table 37*

DESCRIPTION OF TEACHING ABOUT TITHING

Which of the following best describes your denomination's teaching about tithing?

	Canada			U.S.	
	Pastors	Involved Laity	Average Laity	Pastors	Laity
minimum standard of giving	6.0	9.4	9.2	20.5	27.0
one suggestion among many in proportionate giving	76.5	61.4	49.7	76.5	53.6
not regarded as important or useful	17.0	13.3	7.3	1.1	3.4
don't know/ no response	0.5	15.9	33.8	1.9	16.0

* figures in percentages

volved" laity and 16 percent of the lay people in the United States, simply had no idea what the tithe teaching was about.

It seems to have run into some murky modern weather, both in understanding and application.

However, in some smaller denominations such as the Seventh-day Adventist Church, the tithe still has high standing. Among these smaller, more religiously disciplined groups, 63 percent of the membership felt the minimum denominational standard for giving was the tithe, unalloyed and untampered with. Hardly any of them —only six percent—knew nothing about it.

In the study as a whole, people of at least 50

were more inclined to regard the tithe as a minimum denominational standard—32 percent of them—than were people under 50, only 23 percent of them. In congregations of less than 500 members, 25 percent consider the tithe a minimum standard, two-thirds more than the 15 percent in larger churches. Generally, church members in non-metropolitan areas, particularly in the South, uphold the tithe as a minimum more extensively than those in metropolitan areas.

PROMOTIONAL LITERATURE

The "Sermon on the Amount," quipsters call it. The general effort also gets dubbed by various other names, "Commitment Sunday," the "Every-member canvass," the "Annual visitation." In the inner sanctums of church planning, it's called the "Stewardship program," and it involves a wide range of denominationally and interdenominationally published material designed to inform, guide and stimulate the undertaking.

By whatever name, most lay people are aware that the job goes on in their local congregations. In the United States, 66 percent of the laity report such programs, as do 73 percent of the "involved" laity and 64 percent of the average laity in Canada. At least two-thirds of all those reporting the use of such programs say the emphasis is just as much on the allocation of time and talent to God's work as it is on money.

As would be expected, smaller churches aren't as likely to conduct such programs on a regular basis as are the larger churches. In general, however, such programs seemed to have established themselves as a prevailing pattern of operations in the local churches.

But are they getting results? To find out, people were asked various other questions: Had they actually seen any stewardship literature? Had they read it? And how did it affect them? As for the first query, a solid majority of 61 percent of the U.S. laity, 70 percent of the "involved" Canadians and 38 percent of the average Canadians had done so. Nearly all clergy say they see the materials. Approximately two of every three members also have received such information in the past year. This is relatively high coverage, although it still leaves out a third of the people. Somehow, the information didn't get through to them, although the pastors had it with responsibility for distribution.

More tellingly, however, 90 percent of the lay people who received the literature either read it thoroughly or skimmed through it, and 75 percent of the U.S. laity and 80 percent of the Canadians said it had helped in understanding their responsibilities for support of the church.

Some of their comments: "The materials sharpen our concept of certain needs." "It helps, but it makes me feel bad, especially when I know I could do more." "It gave meaning and purpose to what we are doing." "They refresh our minds of needs." "When we found out the budget was in deficit, we started giving more." Others were not so favorably impressed. "You can't change people. Nothing makes them give more." "They irritate me and I give what I want."

Although the predominantly favorable reaction is only subjective, it still indicates a crucial point: that when the promotional material does get through, it reinforces the feelings of members about giving to the church. A third of the members, however, are not getting this help. Between them and the denominational production of the materials, the channels partly have become clogged, apparently at the intermediate point of the local clergy.

When callers pay a visit to people's homes to talk about contributions to the church, most people like it, whether acknowledging it increases their giving or not. Here are some of their comments about it:

"It was welcome." "A nice idea." "Okay." "I enjoyed it. It was nice to have someone from the church." "It was very friendly." "It was a good experience." But a minority voiced qualifications and annoyance. "I enjoy it but my husband is upset by it." "Not much advantage." "I guess it's all right. Maybe older people enjoy it but it's a waste of time to me. There needs to be more friendship in visiting." "The visitors come for money, flit in and out. They should stay longer."

For the most part, however, people found it a pleasant experience even though the majority said they didn't make church contributions because of it but would have done so anyway. About 18 percent said they didn't like it. A heavy majority, 68 percent, said they definitely appreciated it and another seven percent had mixed feelings but were not against it. Clergy were even more enthusiastic, with only eight percent of the U.S. pastors and three percent of the Canadian clergy turning thumbs down on it.

Oddly, however, although 80 percent of the U.S. laity and about 93 percent of the Canadian laity either liked the visit or felt neutral about it, most of them said it had no bearing on their gifts to the church. "No, I would give anyway," said 70 percent of the U.S. laity, 89 percent of the "involved" Canadians and 69 percent of the average Canadians. Even so, most got a satisfaction out of it and felt better about the church.

What seems even more directly significant financially, however, is that 11 percent of the

U.S. laity gave more because of the visit and another two percent gave for the first time. Among Canadians, 20 percent gave more, two percent for the first time. An increase of upwards of 15 percent in giving is no trivial matter in church budget-raising. This, combined with the general boosts reported in member morale, would seem firmly to justify the extensive effort and time that goes into the home calls.

Furthermore, considering the tendency of human nature to insist on self-directing control of decisions and the reluctance to ascribe them to outside influence, there also is a question whether all of those who said they would have given to the church anyhow without the visit actually would have done so.

In any case, the visits yield a predominantly favorable harvest, not just in acknowledged financial improvements for the church, but also in the atmosphere of person-to-person concern and involvement generated among members.

The annual visitation process, as developed in great detail and with high finesse by denominational program planners, involves not just the call but also a variety of procedures, including mailing of literature and letters, showing of films, talks by lay speakers and presentation of program folders describing the church's operations and budget. Since the process has produced documented results when its guidelines are followed fully, the study sought to examine whether the procedure is being adequately used in the churches.

Denominational program developers doubt that it is properly carried out in any given year by more than 10 percent of the local churches. Are such estimates correct? Not necessarily. They seem to minimize the extensive efforts being made by the local churches. Yet, by the limiting terms of full, proper and annual employment of the program, the findings pinpoint no statistical answer. The local approaches, subject to varying circumstances, are too diversified to draw categorical conclusions about it. But it is obvious that full-scale, regular use of all the programed accouterments does remain spotty.

Films are reported used occasionally, annually or more often by about half the U.S. laity and by about a third of the "involved" Canadians and a fourth of the average Canadians. Lay speakers are reported used occasionally or regularly by 71 percent of the U.S. lay people, half of the average Canadians and two-thirds of the "involved" Canadians. Letters and literature are reported seen regularly by about 80 percent of the respondents. Three-fourths of the U.S. laity and nearly half the Canadian laity annually use budget-presentation folders.

Altogether, the various materials come to the attention annually or at least occasionally of more than half the American lay people. The proportion is considerably higher for the larger churches, those of more than 300 members, and those in metropolitan areas than for the smaller congregations and non-metropolitan areas.

The diversified pattern, with churches differing widely in the extent of employment of various media or combinations of them, suggests that a great degree of selectivity goes on in the programs, with clergy choosing resources deemed appropriate to particular congregations. While the denominational output serves as a resource bank, varying frequency and differing emphases on using one kind of material or another appears geared to what seems acceptable to the particular local membership. Most congregations regularly use the program, but rarely all of one in precise conformity to guidelines.

Does it make a difference? That is the crux of the matter. Does it really affect people's giving to the church? About 35 percent of American church members said that indeed, it did. Another 12 percent weren't sure or offered no response. But the rest, 53 percent, felt it had not swayed them, one way or the other. Nevertheless, that a third of the people felt the materials had stimulated their giving attests to a substantial degree of effectiveness. The proportion was slightly higher for members between the ages of 20 and 49, the age of vitality in the church. Clergy even more strongly—55 percent of the

table 38*

EFFECT OF STEWARDSHIP MATERIALS ON GIVING

Do these materials make any difference in your giving?

	yes	no	uncertain	no response
U.S.				
Pastors	44.0	47.0	6.2	2.8
Laity	33.3	54.1	7.9	4.6
Canada				
Pastors	55.0	36.9	5.7	2.4
Involved Laity	29.8	60.5	4.6	5.2
Average Laity	26.1	60.2	5.2	8.6
Total	34.6	53.4	7.4	4.6

* figures in percentages

Canadians and 44 percent of the U.S. clergy—attested to the impact of the materials on contributions, as shown in Table 38.

To most people reporting their generosity enlarged by the materials, they said the reason for it was that the information gave them a fuller insight into church needs, both locally and extending beyond that into denominational work and in the mission field. This is a prime intent of the interpretative and informational material, and that objective is being attained in about a third of the laity and half the clergy, a difference that may be partly due to the fact that a larger share of lay people never see the material.

Aside from the preparatory materials, the decisive point comes with the visit itself. People not only were asked whether they liked being visited by a fellow church member, which most of them do, but whether they thought a "yearly annual visit to collect financial commitments for pledges for next year's budget is a good idea." More than two-thirds of the respondents agreed that it was. Forty-two percent of those asked said they were visited each year. Asked if their particular congregation used that method as a means of obtaining pledges, 64 percent said yes.

Among the third of the people who said visits were not made in their congregations, some cited the use of other techniques such as observance of a special "loyalty Sunday," the holding of "in-church" or "neighborhood" meetings devoted to encouraging financial support of the church. Just as adaptations occurred in the use of preliminary materials, so these modifications and abbreviations are substituted for the visiting process. The alterations are most common in churches of less than 300 members and in nonmetropolitan areas.

But whether or not the regular round of personal visits is the going system, most churches report reliance both on free-will offerings and on pledges for underwriting their budgets. Pledges are signed statements of how much a member intends to give during the coming year. Without this indication of anticipated income, it is virtually impossible for a church to plan any long-range program or even to guarantee that the church will be kept open. A few members still object to pledges (although willingly pledging to pay their rent and utilities bill to keep those services running), but the method has become almost universal in the churches, helping to put their financial planning and accounting on a more rational basis.

While visitation is the most widely used means for enlisting these commitments, a system reported used by 64 percent of the American laity, a rather jolting disparity occurs with another specific question about whether the respondents in churches using the system had themselves been visited in the last two years. Fifty-six percent said no. The figure was even higher among U.S. laity, as shown in Table 39, page 162. Evidently, although their congregations use the system, a lot of people are left out.

Since the nature of the visits and competence of the visitors also have a major bearing on success of the operation, the study took a look at this aspect. About 40 percent of the members reported having served as visitors in seeking financial commitments from fellow members and three-fourths of them said they received some kind of training beforehand. However, only a third attended formally structured training meetings as outlined in denominational procedures. Most of the others received only informal briefings. A few went at the job merely on the basis of written instructions.

table 39*

VISITS TO LOCAL CHURCH MEMBERS FOR PLEDGES

Have you been visited during the past two years by a fellow local church member during a campaign for pledges or commitments for the yearly budget?

	yes	no	don't know no response
U.S.			
Pastors	16.0	84.0	
Laity	31.1	68.1	0.8
Canada			
Pastors	29.4	70.6	
Involved Laity	48.4	51.6	
Average Laity	50.6	47.7	0.7
Total	42.9	56.2	0.9

* figures in percentages

The lack of skilled training is further pointed up by reactions to those who provided it. Most of the visitors who received it said they were trained by other laymen in the congregation, its leaders or the pastor, sometimes a combination of both. A small proportion, 12 percent, were trained by professional fund-raisers and 17 percent by denominational staff members. In scoring the quality of the training, respondents gave much higher marks to the professional fund-raisers and denominational staff members than to fellow laymen and pastors, suggesting that adaptations in the visitation program to substitute local leaders to train visitors may be a drawback.

Despite the indications of weaknesses in the training process, however, a majority of church members said they would be willing to serve as visitors. Such willingness was expressed by 55 percent of the U.S. laity, 61 percent of the "involved" Canadians, and 46 percent of the average Canadian laity. Overall, this is a considerably larger proportion than the 40 percent who said they already have served in that capacity, indicating some available extra manpower. However, about 17 percent of those offering their services qualified their answers by saying "if needed," "if asked" or "if adequately trained."

PLEA FOR PARTICIPATION

In a time when the hugeness and complexity of society seems to swamp the influence of the individual and when the urge for "participatory democracy" breaks out in plea, passion and rage, most American church people say they would be more willing to give to the church if they had more say in how the money is spent and in the shaping of church programs.

Overall, 65 percent of the respondents declare they would give more freely if they could share in program development and 60 percent say they would be similarly encouraged if they had a voice in how their money is spent. These answers augment other replies by a majority saying they think the local church should earmark funds it sends through the denomination for specific purposes.

However, the urge for a local hand in shaping programs and determining the uses of money is even stronger, particularly among U.S. laity.

Seventy-one percent of U.S. pastors and 60 percent of the U.S. laity said people would be inclined to give more if they had a voice in allocating the funds, while 83 percent of the U.S. pastors and 63 percent of the laity foresaw similar results if people had a part in planning programs. Canadians were less inclined to see any benefits in giving people more voice in determining expenditures, but did think it would help if they had a part in program development. The figures appear in Tables 40 and 41.

table 40*

MONEY TO THE CHURCH
DEPENDENT ON VOICE IN ITS USE

People would be more willing to give to the church if they had a voice in the way money is spent.

| | U.S. | | Canada | | | |
	Pastors	Laity	Pastors	Involved Laity	Average Laity	Total
strongly agree, agree or tend to agree.	71.5	60.1	43.8	39.7	48.2	65.3
strongly disagree, disagree or tend to disagree.	28.5	39.6	54.6	58.9	50.2	34.1
no response		.3	1.6	1.4	1.6	.6

* figures in percentages.

Similarly, in a query about whether local churches should earmark funds sent to the denomination for specific uses, only about a third of the laity said no, with about half favoring it and the others being uncertain. In both of these cases, whether in shaping programs and controlling uses of money at home, or in having some say in the destined use of funds sent to the denomination, there is strong, simmering sentiment for a bigger part in the process.

table 41*

MONEY TO THE CHURCH DEPENDENT ON VOICE IN PROGRAM DEVELOPMENT

People would be more willing to give to the church if they had a voice in the way programs are developed.

	U.S.		Canada			
	Pastors	Laity	Pastors	Involved Laity	Average Laity	Total
strongly agree, agree or tend to agree.	83.1	63.4	76.5	51.9	49.9	65.3
strongly disagree, disagree or tend to disagree.	16.9	36.6	23.5	44.3	48.0	34.1
no response	1.0			3.8	2.1	.6

* figures in percentages

"If we knew where the money is going, and we knew it is helping someone, we would give more readily," went one comment about earmarking. Others: "It would give contributors a feeling of more personal relationship and indicate a congregation's evaluation of programs." "Local people should have their desires fulfilled by national agencies." "You would have a closer tie and follow up your money." "The local church should have some say." "A church thus expresses its concerns." "People would feel more involved personally and feel more enthusiastic about giving."

But there also were reasons expressed against

it. "The local church doesn't know the priority of needs." "Nationally they have a much broader picture than we do." "If you are a member of a denomination, you support the family budget with confidence that the leaders usually know better where the needs are." "We should trust our leaders who see both sides and make these decisions."

Despite the diversity of opinion, the findings show a majority of American church people would feel happier about their giving if they had some direct connection, some personal touch, with the spending. This seems to speak an earnest plea, both locally and nationally. In a time when individual humanity seems smothered in the massiveness of social-industrial systems, church people seek some fuller leverage in their churches, the one institution whose principles commit it to attentiveness to the individual person. Its people claim a more active share in the planning, the choosing of alternatives, the direction of the outlays. What's more, if they were allowed that prerogative, they say they would give more generously.

OVERVIEW

A new kind of membership prevails today in American churches, sharp, articulate, capable. It is better educated than ever before. Nearly half the church constituency reports having some college-level education and a fourth are college graduates. All but about 10 percent have had at least some high school work, and three-fourths have completed it. This makes for a more knowledgeable caliber of laity than ever peopled the pews, and they are not there just to pray, obey and pay. They are accustomed to the workaday whirl of productivity and most of them want a corresponding drive and definite direction in the church. They want to be heard.

These are not the quiescent, submissive church flocks of old who accepted unquestioningly every syllable of the institution and its clergy. Yet they exhibit a basic loyalty and dedication both to their traditions and to the Christian cause generally and they see its promise in the most exalted religious terms. But they also bring a hard-headed pragmatism to their dealings with it. They scale their church life in close relation with other demands and other values.

Thirty percent of them had family incomes in 1970 of $14,000 or more, and more than half earned more than $10,000. On the average, they make more than their pastors, and in a culture that has toughened them against slick commercialism and advertising gimmicks, they are not to be maneuvered by superficial promotional campaigns. Most of them report their support of the church is unaffected by the current type of informational programs about it, although they do find the material helpful. Thirty-five percent of them said it had stimulated their contributions.

Similarly, most of them say those intimate, chatty visits in their homes to round up pledges have little to do with the actual amounts they give, although they were pleased to have someone come to talk about it, anyhow. Their responses underline both flaws and strengths in the present stewardship programs, even in the word itself. The members are restless about lingering traces of paternalism, dubious of emotional pitches, but sensitive to backing needs and work that will count and show results that they can see. Most say they would give more willingly if they had a bigger part in determining programs and apportioning expenditures. They may mean it.

6.

peering ahead

"Before the beginning of the next century, Christianity will have disappeared from the face of the earth." Sound familiar nowadays? The forecast was made by the French skeptic, Voltaire, in 1750. About the same time, the famed philosopher David Hume somberly predicted that the church would perish in his generation. Similar forebodings have sounded through the centuries, and the present age also has produced its dirges of churchly doom. The churches are in their "convulsing death throes" with about 10 more years of life, a Canadian bishop said recently.[1] A colleague suggested 50.

In the religious household and out of it, the distress signals flew. Scholars spoke of believers diminishing gradually into a "diaspora" with only a few rugged remnants left here and there, engulfed in a secular sea. Technology, purchasing power and pills were crowding out faith, they said. The church was folding up, crumbling away in the face of pellmell cultural change that demolished traditions, undermined values, homogenized individuals and replaced quality with quantity and prayers with chemicals. In many circles of society, says United Methodist pastor

[1] Anglican Bishop Ralph Dean, 1969 Synod of the Anglican Church of Canada, reported in United Methodist magazine, *Together*, Oct. 2, 1969.

George F. Carter, the church seems "about as useful as a dead cat." [2]

But how do American church members feel about it? Amid all of the publicized laments and handwringing, oddly enough, they retain a cool assurance, detecting no collapse of the foundations. They expect the church not only to hold its own in the years ahead, but as most of them see it, to become even more vigorous, pervasive and influential in the world. With irony in his optimism, a Pittsburgh engineer observed, "When you get to the bottom, you've got to go up."

Indeed, the church did have tough problems. Within its own purview of operations, there were strains, controversy and polarization. The young generation seemed mostly disinterested, scorning the established pomp and protocol and departing in droves, yet still with a devouring appetite for almost any kind of mystical oddity that came along. Clergy grappled with a so-called "identity crisis," wondering just what pastoral oversight meant in these disorderly, rebellious days, and occupational pursuits and community affairs barrelled along with hardly a churchward glance.

Society-at-large appeared on the verge of blowing up much of the time, and the turbulence whipsawed and battered at the church, testing what it stood for. Industrial, military and government power swelled to colossal proportions, and populations shuddered at the devastation left by war and bombs on rustic villages. The smouldering afflictions of racism and ghetto poverty churned in the open and nature reared up in vindictive protest against wanton exploitation and the modern avalanche of pollution.

Inescapably, the turmoil affected the church,

[2] *Together,* April, 1969.

the conflicts and dislocations of the times flooding it with anxieties. Doubt, questioning and apathy seemed to abound both within its ranks and beyond, along with new waves of superstition and fascination with the occult. Many young people cut out, giving up on the "system," withdrawing into the insulated privatism of drugs, communes and esoteric cults.

Pollsters, sampling their regular lists of U.S. residents both in and out of the churches, reported in 1971 that a majority feel the church is headed downhill, losing its influence and shrinking in importance to modern man. The polls also cite waning attendance. Church statistics themselves show that membership growth slowed through the 1960s and into the 70s, along with a lag of income behind the inflationary spiral. Certainly there were ample signs of trouble for the churches.

But inevitably, the making of the future hangs on the hope that is held in it. "In this hope we were saved," St. Paul put it.[3] An old saying goes "Where there is life, there is hope," but it might be put more aptly, "Where there is hope, there is life." And that empowering quality, that dynamo of hope, predominates in the North American churches today.

"The more trouble we have in society, the bigger the job for the church," said a Buffalo, New York customs inspector. "The world has lost its sense of direction and is going to have to turn to the church to find it," said a Dixon, Illinois purchasing agent. Added a San Francisco housewife, "More people are searching for God." "People have gone so far the other way, they're bound to come back," said a Cincinnati lawyer. "Many young people are returning to the

[3] Romans 8:24

church." "It will be less of a show," said a Sanford, Maine pastor, "but actually it will be more vital." "When the world is in trouble, there's one thing that people turn to, and that's the church," said a Richardson, Texas catalogue sales manager. Said a High Falls, New York mechanic's wife, "I'm very hopeful."

These are not the standard voices of the periodic polling systems, but the fresh, representative reflections of the church membership itself. Among believing people, among those who actually make up and hold responsibility for sustaining the church's future, the prevailing mood is not one of dissolution and downfall, but a sense of the church's indispensability, the present urgency of its work and of gathering strength.

Three-fourths of the respondents said the church will be just as important or more so in society in the next 10 years. Only a minority, onefourth, think it will become less important. As shown in Table 42, page 172, half of the people are convinced that the church will become increasingly significant in the coming years, despite the challenges now buffeting it.

As in any broad cross-section, however, there also were notes of discouragement and failure. "People are leaving the church," said the wife of a Boswell, Pennsylvania laborer. "They have other things to do." "Movements are springing up circumventing the church," said a Little Rock, Arkansas assistant road commissioner. A Eugene, Oregon accountant said, "Apathy will negate the church in the next 40 years." "The church is failing because it has not adjusted to change nor made its voice heard in social crises," said the retired dean of an agricultural school in Knoxville, Tennessee. A Calgary, Canada pastor despaired, "We face the complete secularization of the life of our times."

table 42*

IMPORTANCE OF THE CHURCH
IN THE NEXT TEN YEARS

Do you think that the church will become less important, more important, or have about the same importance in society in the next 10 years?

	less important	more important	about the same	no response
U.S.				
Clergy	25.3	55.0	17.9	1.8
Laity	21.4	53.5	23.6	1.5
Canada				
Clergy	23.3	60.9	15.8	
Involved Laity	30.7	23.8	41.1	4.4
Average Laity	35.4	27.5	34.0	3.0
Total	24.4	50.5	23.4	1.7

* figures in percentages

Most of his associates, however, felt definitely otherwise. In fact, Canadian pastors, those tradition-laden clerics with their deep-dyed sense of history and the cyclic nature of cultures, were generally more confident than any other category about the church's future. Sixty-one percent of them said it would be brighter and another 23 percent said it would be just as good. Curiously, however, Canadian lay members were distinctively more downcast about the church's prospects. Nearly a third of them felt it will become less important, a fourth more important, the rest reckoned things will continue about the same.

Among the different races, blacks were the most highly optimistic of all about the church. Sixty-two percent of them expect it to grow in importance, compared to 54 percent of the U.S. whites. In the middle came the Spanish Americans of whom 58 percent anticipate stronger church life ahead. Even though blacks

table 43*

VIEWS OF THE CHURCH'S FUTURE
CLASSIFIED BY AGE

	less important	more important	about the same	no response
Clergy				
20—29 years	22.2	70.4		
30—39 years	23.2	63.4	12.7	0.7
40—49 years	30.1	53.0	16.9	
50—64 years	23.4	53.2	23.4	
65 and older	22.0	36.6	19.5	22.0
Laity				
14—19 years	22.9	47.4	28.0	1.7
20—29 years	20.0	56.8	22.7	0.5
30—39 years	24.4	55.8	18.5	1.3
40—49 years	18.5	57.0	22.9	1.6
50—64 years	21.0	51.3	25.6	2.1
65 and older	24.0	49.3	25.2	1.5

* figures in percentages — U.S. only

registered disappointment in the church in other phases of the study, they apparently see changes in progress that will make it more effective, making them particularly sure of its future.

Younger clergy also are more optimistic than their elders, as shown in Table 43. The age classifications reveal that as a clergyman's age advances, his depression deepens about the coming status of the church. Laity generally reflect an optimistic disposition, but the group between 20 and 49 years old are the most confident of all that the church is headed upward, not down. This age bracket includes those who probably will be most influential in shaping that future.

table 44*

**VIEWS OF CHURCH'S FUTURE
CLASSIFIED BY SIZE OF CONGREGATION**

Members:	less important	more important	about the same	no response
less than 150	20.7	54.2	23.3	1.8
150 — 249	26.1	51.9	20.2	1.7
250 — 299	23.0	51.1	23.9	2.0
300 — 499	24.2	52.7	21.3	1.8
500 — 749	26.9	47.5	24.3	1.3
750 — 1,499	26.3	45.7	26.5	1.5
1,500 and more	22.9	47.0	28.4	1.7

* figures in percentages

Among the varying sizes of congregations, those under 500 members are more likely to be certain of a solid future than are those in the bigger, more impersonal congregations, as shown in Table 44.

But they, too, were more hopeful about it than down in the dumps.

THE REASONS FOR IT

Why do church members feel so extensively secure about the church's future? Their explanations ranged from the idea that troubled conditions themselves tend to intensify religious faith to evidence of increased interest among youth. Others found encouragement in a changing life-style among the younger generation that tends to reject the old "gods" of wealth and technical sciences and to be more open to psychic-spiritual truths. Among the minority who felt the church will become weaker, some blamed misdirected programs and others cited mounting defections among youth. Strangely, the modern stance of young people was seen paradoxically, both as a shortcoming and a promise, as if viewed through contradictory lenses. But mainly, the image was favorable. The reasoning, positive and negative, is reflected in Table 45, page 176.

Pro-and-con comments about the possibilities ahead varied widely. A sampling of them: "I see signs that the church is beginning to rise from its slump and that it's in for an exciting era." "The anti-religious tone in the universities will continue to tear up the churches." "Young people today have more moral convictions and recognize people as people. They will be the leaders of a stronger church." "There is an increased awareness of the spiritual side of life." "I see the

table 45*

**REASONS FOR RESPONSES ABOUT THE
FUTURE OF THE CHURCH**

	Canada			U.S.	
	Clergy	Involved Laity	Average Laity	Clergy	Laity
church is needed	21.8	9.4	7.9	17.3	19.9
increased interest in the church	36.4	23.6	25.8	29.7	22.3
new life-style	2.4	3.3	3.8	8.1	12.4
church dedicated to change	7.2		3.1	6.7	2.6
don't need church	13.3	13.8	15.4	12.5	10.9
ecumenical	0.3		0.5	0.2	0.6
youth lose interest	0.9	19.4	19.9	4.6	8.2
disagree with program direction	3.4	4.2	4.6	4.4	1.9
wait and see	10.6	11.9	7.9	7.6	7.8
other and no response	3.6	14.2	11.1	8.8	13.3

* figures in percentages

church as becoming an unpopular minority, very vocal but with nobody listening." "God intervenes at crucial times to renew his church." "If the church is not going to be more important, then we are going down the drain."

MEANS FOR IMPROVEMENT

If the church is going to advance in modern times, as most members think it will, then there may be better ways of promoting that progress than now are customary. Respondents were asked, "Do you think that your local church could do anything that would stimulate you to give more time or money to the church?" Fifty-eight percent, seemingly satisfied with present procedures, said no. As a Carrollton, Kentucky woman put it, "People are like me, stubborn, and will do as they please no matter what the church does." However, 39 percent said yes, helpful things could be done. Asked to be specific, their answers, as shown in Table 46, focused mainly on beefing up and enlivening the church's program, increasing personal involvement, giving members more responsibility and expanding the church's concern and action on social problems.

table 46*

WAYS IN WHICH PEOPLE MIGHT BE STIMULATED TO BE MORE ACTIVE OR GIVE MORE MONEY TO THE LOCAL CHURCH

	Canada		U.S.	
	Clergy	Laity	Clergy	Laity
no response/ don't know	10.8	5.4	8.4	8.0
give me more responsibility	2.7	14.7	4.1	18.3
increase personal involvement	13.5	18.6	23.8	15.8
more social action	21.6	17.8	31.4	18.4
better programs	40.5	39.5	17.1	30.7
better leadership	2.7	1.6	8.0	2.8
other	8.1	2.4	7.2	6.0

* figures in percentages

Some of the comments: "The church should come out and do more asking for our time and talents." "Greater commitment to local community needs." "Stop being so self-centered." "Be more evangelical." "More social involvement." "We should become more active in the community." "Impress on me that others need my assistance." "Place me in more leadership positions." "The minister should take a more active rôle in personally visiting members." "The church should give responsibility rather than just general recognition." "Pay more attention to youth."

Younger members were more likely to advocate changes than their elders. This was the case for 50 percent of the laity under 30 and 43 percent of those between 30 and 49, the age segment that seemingly forms the backbone of the church. The proclivity for change slackened for older persons, down to one-third for those between 50 and 64 and down to only 15 percent for those over that age.

Pastors, in parallel age sequence but in even greater proportions, felt that potential local innovations and change would strengthen the church. So said nearly two-thirds of those under 30, 54 percent of those in the 30 to 49 bracket, 41 percent of those 50 to 64 and a reduced 32 percent of those 65 or older. The findings disclose that there is a deep vein of common sentiment among clergy and laity regarding possible revamping of the church's modes and also that the clergy is sensitive to those possibilities. But apparently neither group is fully aware of the other's attitudes about it, indicating a lack of candid interaction between them.

This snag in lay-clergy communications also is displayed by the widespread assertions by laymen, particularly those under 50, that it would improve their participation in the church if they had specific tasks to do, but that they haven't been given such assignments. They have an urge for more direct involvement but are waiting for an invitation. On the other hand, pastors also appeal for a more involved laity. The wish is there, on both sides, each group's view seemingly unbeknownst to the other. This again suggests the need for greater person-to-person discussion between pastors and members, especially those on the margins of church activity.

Among those proposing changes, more than a third wanted enriched, more compelling church programs, a particular plea of Canadians. Eighteen percent wanted stepped-up efforts in behalf of social justice and more active involvement in community affairs, and nearly as many wished for more church work to do themselves. The younger laity and clergy, those under 30, displayed the most eagerness for more church action on social conditions. This inclination found stronger support among clergy at all ages than among the laity. Lay people, between 30 and 40, are comparatively more interested in sharpening up the church program than in other possible modifications.

Blacks showed livelier concern for changes than whites, with 50 percent of the blacks declaring renovated church ways would bolster their ties to it. Spanish Americans were even more strongly convinced of this, 79 percent of them. Comparatively, the proportion of whites was only 39 percent.

Differences also showed up between the two countries, with only 29 percent of the Canadian laity and 38 percent of the Canadian clergy feeling the local churches could make alterations that would revitalize participation. The figures were higher in the United States, 48 percent of the clergy and 38 percent of the lay people. In both categories, the impetus for change was 10 percent higher in the United States. Apparently the Canadians are more satisfied with the status quo than their neighbors to the south, or at least less interested in wanting something done.

In both countries, however, a substantial majority felt that nothing could be done to increase their participation. Revealingly, when asked why, most of this group said they already were handling as much church work as possible, so changes would make no difference. In essence, their reaction interposed no objections to

table 47*

REASONS PEOPLE CANNOT BE STIMULATED TO BE MORE ACTIVE OR GIVE MORE MONEY TO THE LOCAL CHURCH

| | Canada | | U.S. | |
	Clergy	Laity	Clergy	Laity
no response	32.6	11.9	23.9	17.3
doing all I can	62.4	48.5	67.0	52.9
personal	2.5	28.1	4.3	22.0
not active		2.3		0.4
don't need church		3.3	0.9	2.5
church not interested in me		1.0	0.4	0.9
leadership		1.0	0.8	0.6
program limited		1.0		0.8
other	2.5	3.0	2.6	2.6

* figures in percentages

change, contending only that it would have no bearing on their already packed schedule. Most others cited a variety of personal interests or problems interfering with church activity. The proportions citing different categories of reasons why they felt change was of no use are shown in Table 47.

Two-thirds of those 30 to 49 said they already are doing all they can at the present time, compared with less than half of those under 30. The younger group obviously feels less absorbed in church business, and offers a potential for church activity not yet exhausted to the extent that it is among older people. The commonest answer among teen-agers on why nothing could be done to augment their participation was simply that they don't need the church. As a Bel Nor, Missouri girl put it: "People are getting into other things. I don't want to have much to do with the church. My parents don't put any pressure on me and I'm allowed to do what I want. I don't think the church could do anything that would influence me. What it says just doesn't reach me."

SUMMARY

In a day when the church seems to have its back to the wall and when many seem ready to scrub it out, church people themselves voice a resoundingly different view. They recognize the restlessness, the instability of the times, even the uneasiness in their own ranks, but at the same time, they're largely calm and confident about the church's future. "The weather looks rough," said a Memphis, Texas farmer, "but you've got to hope or you're licked."

Hope amid tribulation is a running theme of Scripture. Over the storm, it was symbolized of old to Noah. "I do set my bow in the cloud, and it will be a sign of the covenant between me and the earth." [4] Across the somber clouds, the rainbow signalled a brighter day. That reinforcing gleam of hope continued through the ages despite the grimness of the problems. It drew Abraham into a far, unknown country. Out of slavery, it called the Israelites toward freedom and sustained them through desolate desert wanderings. In the midnight of the crucifixion, hope raised its supreme beacon to humanity in the resurrection. Hope is the central watchword for Christians, those "children of promise," [5] as Scripture calls them, following a "God of hope." [6]

By and large, American church people hold to that unflagging hope for the church despite the confusion and trauma that beset it. It will stand, they say, it will increase and shine in the years to come. Somehow, consciously or unconsciously, out of the depths of their heritage, they sense that no matter how sharp the travail, there is always promise ahead. The church has gone through many midnights before, always to emerge renewed, revitalized, refreshed, rallied by men like St. Francis, Luther, Wesley. Throughout history, a secure, stable, unruffled church inevitably has meant spiritual doldrums, inertia, languor. "Woe to those who are at ease in Zion," the prophet warned. [7] It is in times of uneasiness and disturbance that quickening comes; in the times of darkness, tumult and uncertainty, believing people look up and hope.

Church people today hold to that firm expec-

[4] Genesis 9:13
[5] Romans 9:8
[6] Romans 15:3
[7] Amos 6:1

tation, finding promise in the very upheavals and nihilism of the day. They also take heart in the young people, a generation dubious of church organization, but disenchanted with materialism and hungering for the transcendent. Their search sometimes takes bizarre forms, their gurus, astrology, contemplation and fasting, but it is a search, nevertheless, a reaching for ultimate meaning, a yearning for faith. Church members sense that same hunger rising in the population generally. This and other signs, some of them troubling in themselves alone, are seen as heartening for the church's future.

Most of its members recognize no necessity for changes in it to deepen their commitment, particularly those who already are heavily involved. But a substantial minority, particularly the younger members and blacks, are convinced that changes would serve to heighten their participation and strengthen the church. Most of them want programs made more challenging. Some feel sidelined and want to be drawn into more church responsibilities, while others urge greater efforts in dealing with social problems in the community-at-large.

But whatever their prescriptions for change, they're not despairing of the church, nor giving up on it. They're confident about it and many are eager to shoulder more work in it. They trust the future. It always belongs to those who believe in it and take responsibility for it.

7.

the implications

With all the parts of the puzzle spread out on the table, you sit there, not knowing just how to fit them together. Some of them look peculiar, even contradictory, some of them graceful and pleasing, some jarring, others hauntingly suggestive like ink blots in a Rorschach test. Where to put them? What to make of them?

Research data always is like that, the separate pieces intriguing but baffling in isolation, yet potentially loaded with meaning in conjunction with the other parts, each of which also remains obscure without the rest.

It is a little something like life itself, trying to get its fragments together into some kind of integrated perspective. Just as doing that always remains an unfinished objective, so this study seeking a more balanced realistic image of the church in our time must also remain only a step toward trying to accomplish it.

Truth in our human pilgrimage is never a goal entirely won, but the pursuit of it is what keeps the going interesting and worth the effort. Sometimes, too, the glimmerings that do come through can add some bit of authenticity to the gradual, unending, seesaw task of building fuller understanding of our lives.

The church today has its ills and undoubtedly always has had them, but the findings of this report substantiate some of the particular ailments now confronting it. Uncovering them doesn't cure them, or prescribe how. But, as hoped in this case, the mere gathering of facts and analysis of them can contribute to dealing with them.

In the same way, when a person feels out of sorts, the first procedure is to try to find out what's wrong. A blood count analysis will tell if he has anemia, but won't tell what should be done about it. Similarly, this study brings out some afflictions in the church, but provides no plan to remedy them. However, merely locating the problem zones is in itself a necessary antecedent for developing the solutions.

The patient in this instance was the far-flung body of American Protestantism, its manifold, heterodenominational human fabric, high and low, its ministers and members across the continent. The taking of their pulse showed a hardy beat in modern church life, but it also showed up some erratic jumps and lapses that hurt.

A basic problem that emerged is simply one of understanding—between clergy and laity, between working and passive members, between local congregations and denominations, between theology and its imperatives. This doesn't mean any yawning discord between the various segments, but that they remain partly disconnected and often misapprehend one another. They aren't sufficiently or accurately combined for mutual support and fuller health. To some extent at least, it is a communications gap.

American clergymen, immersed in their field yet plagued by fears that religion makes little difference to a modern technical-minded generation, say repeatedly that the chief hindrance to church life is simply that the church is no longer considered important. They say that is why people lose interest, why they abandon the church. It is the topmost obstacle, they say, overshadowing many others, the main malaise. But those who purportedly are infected with it, the people themselves, blithely disown it and admit no symptoms of it. They subordinate it to a virtual inconsequentiality, citing a half dozen other major difficulties, none of them questioning the church's stature and significance in the present-day atmosphere. Somehow, out of their differing rôles, the clergy has misinterpreted the laity's mood about the matter and lay people have not been sufficiently sensitive to their pastors' agonies about it to offer much reassurance.

The ache in the clergyman's outlook about the diminished standing of the church constitutes a painful morale conflict for him, since his vocation hinges on the church's importance. Yet he's convinced that the estimate on which he staked his career no longer exists in society, leaving him in a forlorn undertaking which he assumes is considered archaic. A distressing state. Yet the world of the laity to which he attributes this attitude demonstrates over and over that it does not agree, which might be good for him to know.

This is only one of the points at which misconceptions occur. Most clergymen keenly feel that church attempts to apply principles of the Gospel to controversial social problems antagonizes members, but that it nevertheless should be done in adherence to the scriptural mandate. Similar impressions, probably caught from the clergy, also prevail in denominational leadership. However, repudiating this thesis, most lay members maintain that the denominations not only have the right to speak out on contemporary social issues, such as racial justice and war, but have a duty to do so. They see this primarily as a denominational role, however, not that of the local congregation.

The worried but conscientious misinterpretations among the clergy and other church leaders about it is part of the result of the institutionalization of the Gospel, making it automatic to weigh the popular effect of actions before taking them. But the findings of the study show that the "straws in the wind" about it have been miscalculated to a large extent, that the measuring has perhaps depended on too limited a range of church viewpoints. Certainly there always are dissenters whenever the church moves into troubled areas, but while the dissenting voices may be loud, a different word comes from the church-at-large.

Most lay people also support ecumenical activities and look favorably on the principal U.S. agency of interdenominational cooperation, the National Council of Churches. Because of its standing policy of speaking out about the Gospel's implications regarding contemporary issues, it has been the common "whipping boy" of those opposed to church social action. However, only the scantiest fraction of lay people resent its work, and most approve of it. Actually, the study shows the clergy are more prone to censure it than the laity. In doing so they often contend they are expressing the membership's attitude, which turns out not to be so.

Another bugaboo tumbled by these findings is the idea that members widely withhold contributions when they don't like some particular church program or position. Only a scattered few, six out of every hundred, have done it, although a substantial minority would not foreclose the right of others to do so if they feel it is conscientiously necessary. But the vast majority of church people find it objectionable within the diversified unity of the church to take financial reprisals against it because of individual reservations about isolated aspects.

The clergy, who have extensively and warningly ascribed the tactic to lay members, actually have resorted to it just as much themselves. While this is only a handful in both cases, the practice is no more characteristic of lay people than of their pastors. In fact, the clergy are more apt to specify grounds for doing it than ordinary members who generally have not thought of it in such definite terms. It is just not on their minds.

Beyond getting the record straight on these functional matters, however, the strong, steady note that sounded throughout this study was the overwhelming, unshaken dedication to classic Christian beliefs, a plea for fuller teaching of them, and an insistence that they be plainly proclaimed in the cause of evangelizing the nations and winning others to faith in Christ.

Members regard this as the church's prime responsibility. Their massive consensus about it comes at a time when many church thinkers have concluded that the message must be qualified and reformulated to suit the modern mentality and presented with less absolute certitude in a more modest style. But the people, with all their up-to-the-minute sophistication and savvy, feel otherwise. They firmly uphold the historic doctrines and want deeper instructional nurture in them. In part, this represents a plea for better adult Christian education, at present a hit-or-miss aspect of much congregational life, often amateurish or absent altogether, leaving many adult members to get by on a kind of kindergarten theology remembered from elementary Sunday schools. They want a fuller fare of spiritual food and sustenance of the Gospel. They want it preached and taught and spread.

"The church must return to the preaching of the Gospel," declared an Ohio salesman. "It is the only way we can be effective."

The sentiment was echoed over and over again. To clergymen worried that the church is losing prominence in modern life and their sometimes resultant hesitancy about trying to get the verities of faith across to presumably deaf ears, the call from the people for vigorous, decisive teaching of the Word might help restore more mettle to the ministry.

A sizable block of people maintain that enlarged personal responsibilities in the church and sharper, livelier programing would strengthen their identification with the church. Others, especially among the younger clergy and lay members, so vital to the church's future, want it to move increasingly into community affairs and into tackling social problems. They insist this will stimulate participation and project Christian ethics into public thinking. These suggestions essentially reflect an appeal for upgraded and expanded dissemination of the church's message.

Despite the people's firm avowals of belief along with their assertion that devotion to God impels their financial support of the church, the two dimensions show little congruity in actual practice. Although members generally earn more than the clergy, the pastors more closely match their giving habits with their theology, contributing to the church an average amount triple that given by lay members. Both groups say the lure of other "good things" is the main thing deflecting support from the church, but the impact of that urge seems greater on the laity than on the clergy—another hint of the need for fuller adult religious education.

Various causes of frustration turned up among the lay people. They would like a greater voice in congregational affairs, in devising programs and deciding where funds are used. They delight in being visited and listened to, but a majority of them report they get missed in the regular rounds of visitation. They feel they aren't realizing the full potentials of church life, that the answers to elemental needs reside in it, but aren't being supplied in a wholly satisfying way. Many of them, particularly those only peripherally involved, would like to serve more actively, but await being asked by the "pillars" or pastor, who themselves claim a dearth of such willingness. It is there, untapped.

There are other obvious bottlenecks in the church's operation, usually reflecting clogged communications. Denominational literature reaches the pastors, but only about two-thirds of the lay people ever see it. Most of those who do examine it say it helps them understand the broader purposes and reasons for supporting those purposes. A third say it affects the actual amounts they give. But many have no chance to know how it might influence them.

In the makeup of the congregations, the study consistently discloses a kind of stratification of attitudes, often by ages. A middle-range group, between 30 and 59, reflect the greater flexibility, a sympathy both for the reforming, activist passions of the young and for the values of order and stability cherished by the older members.

The wide extent of selectivity exercised by the congregations in using denominationally recommended programs displays a need for varying materials, geared to churches of varying sizes and capabilities and for varying age and interest groups. Since most denominations lack the resources for developing such a range of materials, however, further ecumenical cooperation might be necessary to provide them.

The frequently blurred understandings between clergy and laity indicated needed improvements on both sides. Since the pastors often misinterpret the lay people's views and concerns, changes in clerical training to give ministers a wider background in lay experiences might help clear up the relationships and enable them better to serve their congregations. Steps for accomplishing this are now being taken by some seminaries with students spending time in the secular arena to get a better sense of it. At the same time, the members want a deeper nurture in theology, and imply a concrete need for it in some of their dealings with the church.

The urgency for fuller intercommunication and sharing of insights and information shows up repeatedly in other areas, suggesting the continuing need for broadening and opening up the process at all levels. Both pastors and members express a yearning for greater awareness of their hopes, feelings and problems. Many pastors, while being interviewed, sometimes in a pent-up release of emotion, voiced feelings that the denominational leadership seems to care little about them or their problems, another aspect of their loneliness. But lay people, too, plead to be heard, listened to, visited in their homes, without ulterior motives, which also is part of the need for clearer, expanded communications.

Despite the pangs and inadequacies, however, American church people affirm their joy of life, their sense of ultimate purpose in it and appreciation for the church. They believe it is destined for greater days in spite of the forces pitted against it, that a new spring beckons, a sturdier future. They do not want the church to retreat from the fray, to withdraw into cultic preoccupation focused mainly on itself and its inner circle. This kind of self-absorption has always weakened Christianity, submerging it in ritual introversion. Its historic, sustaining hallmark always has been its reach beyond its own hallowed sanctuaries. And that is what its American members want, that the church concentrate on sowing the seed in wider fields, on calling a wavering civilization to faith, on being about its mission.